Acclaim for *Be Quiet, Be Heard*

"Unlike most authors of books on communication, Glaser and Glaser have chosen to present conceptual frameworks instead of just feeding the reader canned formulas. Then, they've gone an important step further by showing how to apply their concepts—something rarely seen in books that contain theories. This is a winning combination and the reader reaps the benefits."

—Jerry I. Porras, Stanford Business School, and co-author of
Built to Last: Successful Habits of Visionary Companies

"This delightful and substantive book is an important contribution at this time. Everywhere people are struggling to communicate, and even losing heart that good communication is possible. Under the Glasers' wise and clear guidance, we can take heart. If we follow any of these practices that they so well describe, we can develop the skills necessary to turn to one another again."

—Margaret J. Wheatley, author of Leadership and the New
Science *and* Finding Our Way: Leadership for an Uncertain Time

"When asked what most needs improvement in today's business school graduates, the corporate leaders who comprise advisory boards at leading business schools point to oral and written communication skills, hands down. Susan and Peter Glaser have written a persuasive book that will make a meaningful difference in improving the development of effective communication skills of business managers."

—Mark Zupan, Dean
William E. Simon Graduate School of Business
University of Rochester

"To create a successful mass-market product like the X-Box, you need a high-powered team of experts from multiple disciplines. Unfortunately, left in their 'natural' state, such teams often prefer to pontificate, digress at will and compare egos on every occasion. The Glasers' research-based insights into workplace dynamics have helped me re-focus my team. Bickering is now rare, morale is up, and the product demos are earning rave reviews from the press!

"The Glasers' models are so effective that at first I wondered if applying them would be considered cheating. I quickly dropped that thought when I realized that my team was delivering better quality work, feeling more motivated, and thanking me for being so much more thoughtful, helpful, and fair!"

  —Michal Bortnik, Program Manager
   Xbox Live
   Microsoft

"As a Chief Executive in the United Kingdom of a large public-sector organization of 20,000 employees, I am recommending this book to employee-development staff so that they may apply it throughout the whole workforce.

"Very few of us are naturally excellent communicators. The Glasers remind us through their straightforward flexible guidelines and frameworks that it is only when we are silent and listen that our own voices will be heard.

"I recommend this book to all managers and professionals who realize that by improving their communication, they will enrich the culture of their organization and have an overall impact on performance."

  —Tom Aitchison, Chief Executive
   The City of Edinburgh Council
   Edinburgh, Scotland

"Effective communication is complex and this book doesn't pretend it to be otherwise. But through analysis of its component parts, readers will easily grasp and implement its essential principles. Those principles are well supported by research findings and case studies that draw on corporate, professional, and personal environments. With an engaging narrative style and a warm sense of humor, Susan and Peter Glaser translate their decades of experience in this field with convincing authority."

>—*Jim Elvey, CEO*
>*Local Government Managers Association National*
>*Melbourne, Australia*

"Finally a no-gimmick, effective skill-building guide for a world that desperately needs to communicate better. Instead of typical business-speak techniques, we learn practical relationship-building communication tools."

>—*Jackson Steele, Training Manager*
>*State of Alaska*

"The Glasers take a 'client-centered' approach to business communication. Instead of titling a chapter 'how to run effective meetings,' they teach collaboration. When they teach public speaking, they take stage-fright straight on and give practical steps for how to overcome it. This is a comfortable and comforting book that will enhance the effectiveness of every young professional who reads it."

>—*David Robinson, Lecturer in Marketing*
>*Haas School of Business*
>*University of California, Berkeley*

"This is the type of book that you don't read once. It will serve as an outstanding reference guide for those interested in reaching agreements and improving their communication."

>—*Paul Lanspery, Deputy General Manager*
>*San Diego County Water Authority*

"Susan and Peter are perennial favorites over the past ten years as presenters at the International City/County Management Association's Annual Conferences, and one look at this book explains why the Glasers receive the highest possible participant evaluations year after year. Their work is fresh, practical, and immediately applicable. Their humor, knowledge, life experience, and ability to connect real solutions to real people make this book unique, innovative, and invaluable."

> —*Felicia Logan, Director of Professional Development*
> *International City/County Management Association*
> *Washington, DC*

Be Quiet, Be Heard is an easy-to-read practical guide to handling awkward business, family and relationship conflicts. Day-to-day examples allow the reader to benefit from clear, real-life advice. This book should be a must at the front of every manager's bookshelf."

> —*Rod Titcombe, Chief Executive*
> *Manawatu District Council, Feilding, New Zealand, and*
> *President, New Zealand Society of Local Government Managers*

"Presented in an entertaining, simple, and straightforward manner, this book moves beyond the intellectual and shows how to live communication day to day, relationship to relationship. The lessons are fundamental, foundational, and need to be practiced continuously."

> —*Karen Shimamoto, Forest Supervisor*
> *Fremont-Winema National Forests*

"An essential and timely piece."

> —*Fariborz Pakseresht*
> *Deputy Chief Administration Officer*
> *Oregon Department of Human Services*

"I was carried from one page to the next as I gleaned many concepts and strategies that are so relevant to my everyday work life, as well as my personal life. I see this as a 'how to' manual that one almost wants to carry around to help with those daily communication challenges. Great tactics are presented, all the way from handling conflict to giving a public speech. This book is one valuable suggestion after another. What a great way to synthesize years of experience and knowledge into one location."

—Wynelle J. Huff, Ph.D., Vice President
Adventist Medical Center

"The Glasers poignantly remind managers that we are the message, and that meaningful management and leadership are based upon our communication skills. This book illustrates a new path for significantly improving outcomes in any organization, through harnessing the energy of communication."

—David H. Ready, City Manager
Palm Springs, California

"For a number of years, our government has benefited from the Glasers' experience and teachings. The application of their principles and skills has transformed our organizational culture and improved both service delivery and internal efficiencies. In this book, the Glasers have distilled their message into a practical and readable volume. The information has been refined over years of hands-on practice with a wide array of public and private organizations, yet it is fresh and timely. Numerous real-life examples bring the theories and models into context for practical application."

—Donna Pierce, Deputy City and Borough Manager
Juneau, Alaska

"Through the guidance that Susan and Peter have provided, I can take accountability for my communication and make it more productive. It definitely will help me in my day-to-day interactions and allow me to influence my organization to move toward a culture where communication is a principal value. This book has definitely given me a new mantra, one to help me succeed in my personal and business life."

—*Jim Sears, Director of Public Works*
Marion County, OR

"The Glasers have done a wonderful job of capturing their hallmark approach to leadership."

—*Eurial (E.T.) Turner, Staff Asst. to the Deputy Chief for*
Programs, Legislation, and Communication
United States Forest Service, Washington, DC

"I found the book to be very practical, easy to read and follow. The use of real examples made the lessons easy to understand and identify with. Also, having examples from work, home, and family made the skills seem more usable. We need to look at clear communication as a life skill, not just a work skill. When this book comes out I will use it with my HR staff for developmental reading."

—*Mary Neidig, Human Resources Director*
Lane Transit District

"The Glasers are masterful trainers. They share their insights and strategies in such a straightforward and common-sense way that I was able to put them to use and see the difference right away. Communication and collaborative problem solving improved greatly at our school as a result of putting the Glasers' transforming insights and techniques to work."

—*Pam McComas, Associate Head*
The Catlin Gabel School, Portland, OR

Dedication

With love, respect, and gratitude to Meegan
and Sam, our daughter and son. You have
been our teachers, our mentors, and our best
friends. You bring innovation to our business
and joy to our lives.

Acknowledgements

To the leaders who agreed to be interviewed for this book. We thank you for so graciously and generously sharing your time and ideas so others can learn from your insights.

Tom Aitchison—Mayor, City of Edinburgh, Scotland; Dave Frohnmayer—President, University of Oregon; John Haughom—Senior Vice President, Peace Health Medical Systems; David Illig—President, Litigation Psychology; Gary Lawhead—Superintendent, Oregon Youth Authority—MacLaren Youth Correctional Facility; Michael Long—Project Delivery Manager, Oregon Department of Transportation; David Marsing—Vice-President/General Manager of Technology and Manufacturing, Intel Corporation; Cheryl Miller—Chief Executive, East Sussex County Council and President of SOLACE (Society of Local Authority Chief Executives and Senior Managers), Great Britain; Wayne Norrie—CEO and Minister of Culture of Hitachi, New Zealand; Norm Smith—President, The Ford Family Foundation; Butch Swindells—Ambassador, U.S. Embassy, New Zealand.

To Layla Yarr, our business manager and life assistant. Your amazing ability to create a foundation of structure and order in an atmosphere of love and ease makes every day a joy.

To our clients and students since 1971. It is you who have brought us to where we are. We thank you for supporting us, challenging us, and celebrating our work. We remain committed to surpassing your expectations.

To the late Gerald M. Phillips, our advisor and mentor, whose gifted intellect and keen wit drew us to study the science and art of human communication.

Be Quiet, Be Heard:
The Paradox of Persuasion

by

Susan R. Glaser, Ph.D.

Peter A. Glaser, Ph.D.

with Arlene Matthews

Table of Contents

What Do You Mean, Be Quiet?
An Introduction

In our three decades as communication researchers and consultants, we have become convinced that successful communication depends on one all-too-elusive ability: to really listen. That's why we titled this book as we did. When we say "Be quiet," we mean: Quiet your mind's conversation. Stop planning your next response. Stop defending yourself against what your critic is saying. Be still, on every level—and just listen!

Senator Jordan, like every U.S. Senator, presides over two internal organizations: a state staff, which handles constituent issues, and a Washington, D.C., organization, which focuses on legislation. Each staff organization, although passionately committed to their senator, has its own priorities.

The state staff group had organized a speaking engagement for the senator with state labor leaders one Thursday night. That morning, and without warning, the D.C. staff cancelled that event in favor of a presentation to local Chamber of Commerce leaders. The speech to eager labor loyalists was cancelled, and the state staff was embarrassed and angry. Bad feelings ensued between the two groups and communication between them all but ceased. Each group began to believe that the other was sabotaging its agenda. Both lost sight of their ultimate mission: to support the senator.

Ann, the director of Public Works in a large Midwest city, is furious with Jim, the Parks Department director. The Department of Parks scheduled an outdoor concert, but notified Public Works so late that extra contract personnel had to be hired at considerable additional expense to the city. Ann is incensed and fires a caustic e-mail to Jim—and copies the city manager. Jim is outraged that Ann didn't have the courtesy to discuss the problem face to face without involving their boss. Now, the only communication transpiring between Ann and Jim is accusation, blame, and recrimination.

Joyce is a 57-year-old baby boomer and senior vice president of an advertising firm. Last month, she asked Bob, a 35-year-old account executive, to meet an important client at 5:00 on Wednesday night. Since this was the same night as his son's soccer game, Bob called the client and rescheduled the appointment for the following Monday. Joyce was livid. She felt that Bob had put an important contract at risk for frivolous reasons. Even though the client did not complain about the rescheduling, Joyce remained upset and gave Bob fewer high-profile assignments. Their relationship became strained, although Bob was not sure why.

When communication goes awry, the result is often retreat. But communication abhors a vacuum, and so this avoidance is filled with negative assumptions and ill will. If the silence is broken, it is too often packed with the relentless noise of people making their own points over and over again. One sad truth remains: no one is really listening to anyone else.

In over thirty years of training leaders and innovators around the globe to make themselves understood and to facilitate communication throughout their organizations, we've often referred to this quote from Aristotle:

The fool persuades me with his reasons, the wise man persuades me with my own.[1]

Why is this true? Because to be wise is to know that nobody likes hearing from the self-absorbed. (In fact we all dread it, don't we?) The wise make far greater inroads by understanding what others desire and require before they proceed.

How can any of us know exactly what sorts of messages others need to hear in order to become receptive? The answer is simple: we are quiet and we listen. Paradoxically, it is only then that we can be heard.

Listening is the foundation for reaching agreement. It allows information to get out into the open. It also builds relationships. Overwhelmingly, we are attracted to people who listen to us well. When things go wrong in any relationship, the first factor to consider is: Are we still listening? When listening stops, it's unlikely that anything else will retrieve the relationship. Once genuine listening is established, all things are possible.

In *Be Quiet, Be Heard*, we have taken our thirty years of consulting and research with thousands of different organizations—and compiled what we have learned. Our models, developed over time, represent proven methods for transforming conflict and increasing cooperation in all sorts of groups—large corporations, small family businesses, government agencies, even family systems—by changing their "culture." Research shows that a strong organizational culture—employee involvement, direct communication, high-functioning teamwork—has an enormous impact on bottom-line issues such as company profits, sales, and customer satisfaction.[2] To use a disturbing example, the Challenger space shuttle disaster may have been caused by faulty "O" rings, but the real cause was faulty communication within the organization. Regretfully, some NASA engineers had grave concerns about the "O" rings, but their voices were not heard.

Though our focus in this book is on improving the communication culture in organizations, these same principles apply to families and other social systems. We have used professional and personal relationship examples—just as we do in our workshops—to help readers relate to and understand our models. We've found that the kinds of skills that transform workplaces do carry over to people's individual relationships. Our communication models can be practiced equally well with family and friends as with bosses and employees.

Be Quiet, Be Heard rejects canned formulas that leave little room for adaptability. When people try to speak using a pre-packaged sound byte, others see right through the one-size-fits-all technique. In lieu of staid formulas, we offer models that provide broad, flexible guidelines and progressive steps that can be easily adapted to specific communication challenges. Effective communication is indeed an art, but it is an art that can be accessed through science. Our models provide a framework (the science part) around which individuals can earnestly wrap their own words and nonverbal behaviors in their own style (the art part).

Using the models presented in *Be Quiet, Be Heard*, readers will learn what the most persuasive communicators already know:

- **Communication has a hidden dimension.** The impact of a message is often different from its intent.
- **Perceptions require reality checks.** We assume we know what others are trying to say, but often we're wrong.
- **Conflict and criticism generate real breakthroughs.** There are seeds of agreement in every disagreement.
- **Unspeakables have to be spoken.** It's the avoidance of delicate issues and sensitive subjects that creates distance.
- **Persuasive performance transforms the performer.** Focusing on how listeners can best absorb the message generates the ability to effortlessly connect with them.

- **Great speakers have anxiety—and, they embrace it.**
  They use their anxiety as the "juice" that transforms fear
  into enthusiasm.
- **Real power is power through people—not over them.**
  In group settings, influential communicators are cata-
  lysts, drawing out valuable contributions from all.
- **Gratitude must be gracefully extended—and accepted.**
  Praise leads others to repeat the good they've done; spe-
  cific praise motivates them to generate more creative and
  consistent achievement.
- **Synthesis is the height of the art.** The ability to integrate
  skills is a crucial skill in its own right.

Be Quiet, Be Heard expands on each of these ideas so that readers
can understand them not as mere intellectual concepts, but as practical
strategies that can quickly be incorporated into everyday life. Unlike
learning, say, how to play the drums or how to rock climb, no special
equipment or location is required to begin to practice these concepts.
We do, however, stress that what we present in these pages is an action
learning program.

Action learning links theory and practice, and is meant to result in
immediate application of lessons learned. We invite you, as you read, to
begin engaging in the necessary self-analysis and to start observing the
effects your communication has on others. We also invite you to keep an
open mind and a constructive attitude as you try each of the principles
that will help you to master the science and the art of persuasion.

Chapter One

Creatures of Habit

About the time most of us were a year old, we associated a sound with an object and uttered our first word: *dog, bubble, ball, milk, kitty, cracker.* Mom and Dad rejoiced, clapped their hands, and urged us to say it over and over. Pretty soon we added a second word, concocting a rich and ingenious phrase—*dog come, bubble go, cracker yum*—that warranted yet more parental cooing and perhaps even a phone call to grandma (who said she always knew there was genius in the family).

Alas, for most of us, the ability to communicate with this kind of impact went straight downhill from there.

The acquisition of language is a human rite of passage equally thrilling for all who achieve it and all who witness it. To watch a small child move through simple nouns and basic phrases to free-flowing sentences and, ultimately, full-fledged dialogues is to be reminded what a rich and complex gift our species has been given. Yet very few of us make the most of it. Although nearly all of us learn to speak—and pretty competently, at that—few of us ever learn to communicate effectively.

Neglected Teachings

The fact that so many of us are communication challenged is understandable. In 1936, when Dale Carnegie published his classic work, *How to Win Friends and Influence People*, he cited studies done by the Carnegie Institute for the Advancement of Teaching and the Carnegie Institute of Technology. These studies revealed that about 15 percent of career success and financial rewards were attributable to specialized knowledge in one's field. The other 85 percent was due to skill in "human engineering"—i.e., the ability to relate well to people. In 1995, Daniel Goleman, renowned psychologist, author, and researcher in the area of emotional intelligence (EQ), attributed 80 percent of adult success to EQ, which encompasses much the same terrain. Carnegie lamented: "Wouldn't you suppose that every college in the land would conduct courses to develop the highest-priced ability under the sun?" Colleges did not teach "people skills" in 1936, nor in 1995, and—incredibly—they do not do so today. And though we all intuitively understand that possessing "people skills" will afford us both financial rewards and increased personal fulfillment—we're often hard-pressed to think of people who possess such skills in order that we might learn from them.

To say our world is short on effective communication is not to say people don't talk. Talk we've got. Our airwaves reverberate with it. A quick Sunday morning spin around the TV dial yields a talkfest of newsmakers and commentators—shouting heads—spewing partisan politics, accusations, and innuendos. But it doesn't take an advanced degree to see that no one is really listening to anyone else, or even seriously hoping that their own words will convince their opponents. What people are doing is waiting—barely waiting, at that—to pounce on the first pause and fill it with their own words.

Are our personal lives any different? When is the last time most of us actually changed someone else's mind or—far more radical—allowed our own minds to be changed during a conflict with family or friends? Most of us long ago fell into habits that stifle true give-and-take dialogue. We may yak incessantly, but while doing so we're also going out of our way to dodge conflict and to avoid sensitive subjects that raise emotional red flags. Often, we let our friendships and even our most loving and intimate relationships flounder, or fail completely, rather than face the once-small matters that have blossomed into "unmentionables."

If and when conflict does arise, in spite of our efforts to avoid it, we react to others defensively. We fold our arms across our chest and we close ourselves off to the possibility that *maybe somebody else has a point*. Our minds are already made up.

How about in the workplace? Here problems stemming from poor communication practices cost American businesses billions each year in lost work time, lawsuits, and unrealized productivity. Those problems include inadequate conflict resolution, misunderstandings and misinterpretations of policy, and lack of support for employee feedback.

No one doubts, in theory, that effective communication in all directions—upward, downward, and laterally—can help any organization improve its members' morale and its overall results. In fact, a Watson Wyatt ™ Worldwide study linking communication and financial performance showed that organizations that communicate effectively dramatically outpace organizations that don't.[3] Among its key findings:

- A significant improvement in communication effectiveness was associated with a 29.5 percent increase in market value.
- Companies with the highest levels of effective communication experienced a 26 percent total return to shareholders from 1998 to 2002, compared to a minus 15 percent return experienced by firms that communicate least effectively.
- Organizations that communicate effectively were more likely to report employee turnover rates below or significantly below those of their industry peers.

Despite such extraordinary bottom-line evidence, few in the workplace have the courage to accept and benefit from criticism, to collaborate effectively, or to influence anyone else's plans or priorities without pulling rank. We go out of our way to avoid opening up "cans of worms," generally saying only what is required to maintain the status quo.

Courageous Communication

The problem at work, at home, or in any social circumstance is that, when we talk about nothing, nothing ever changes. Status quo communication is communication for the chicken-hearted. Courageous communication, on the other hand, has the power to change virtually any situation or relationship for the better.

In order to be courageous, we must embrace conflict as opportunity. We must face rather than flee the tough issues, understanding that **trust—the foundation of positive and productive relationships—is a *byproduct* of communication rather than a *prerequisite* for it.** But in order to do all this, most of us must undo the habits of a lifetime.

We said earlier that effective communication is a learned behavior. Ineffective communication is also learned. Of course it's not as if someone sat us down and said, "Here's how to ignore your wife's criticism or dodge a confrontation with your boss." Rather, we learned from observing and interacting with others exactly how such things are done. We absorbed the lessons of nonengagement gradually, never realizing what it was that we were doing.

But habits are only inscrutable to those who aren't paying attention. If we make it a point to observe our own communication patterns over the course of a week—or, in many cases, even a day—we'll notice how consistently and how deftly we tune others out so that we can preserve our own ideas, opinions, and judgments.

The Dropout Syndrome

That said, a cautionary note is in order. There's always an inherent danger in admitting we've got a bad habit. Once we do, we may feel compelled to alter it immediately. This sort of all-or-nothing approach doesn't work, and can prove so traumatic it discourages us from trying to change anything about ourselves, in any way, ever again.

Every January, for example, millions of people across the country make New Year's resolutions to join health clubs and get in shape. Unfortunately, many are so unable to curb their enthusiasm for transforming themselves that they begin working out in every conceivable way at every possible hour. They run on treadmills, ride stationary bikes, lift weights, swim laps, and take every level of aerobics, Pilates, and yoga class. Within days they're very, very sore and moving quite a bit more slowly. Within a few weeks they're less and less in evidence at the gym; and within a few months they're gone. In fact, health clubs estimate that 90 percent of members who sign up in January stop working out by April.[4]

In an attempt to instantaneously replace a habit of nonactivity with its extreme opposite, the resolution makers created a shock to their systems. Then, in a retreat from distress, they ended up right back where they began.

We've always advised those with whom we work to approach personal change slowly and respectfully. To focus on "breaking" a habit is to end up with, well, something broken—and nothing more. A habit will recede, slowly but permanently, when it is remade into another, more productive habit. No one learned to talk in one fell swoop, and no one will become a persuasive communicator that way, either. Being courageous is important, but courage without skill and preparation has an overwhelming tendency to backfire.

Those who wish to change permanently will know they're perfectly normal when they observe themselves going through four specific feeling stages: *phony, uncomfortable, comfortable,* and *natural.* The first two stages should be no cause for discouragement.

Feeling Phony

What do we mean by feeling phony? The word "phony" has such negative connotations. The dictionary defines it as "not genuine" or "putting on a show." But when any of us attempts something for the very first time, isn't that the way it feels?

People who work out on a regular basis can probably remember what it was like the first time they put on workout gear. They looked in the mirror, saw a reflection in spandex shorts staring back, and thought: *Who the heck is this?* All mothers and fathers can probably recall the day they initially found themselves alone with their firstborn and thought: *Wait, wait, when are the real parents going to show up?* Likewise, most leaders can likely recall the first time they were tasked with directing a project or group and felt like they were "impersonating" an authority figure.

Throughout this book, we'll be asking you to perform a number of behaviors that are counter-intuitive. At various times, as a part of the process of unraveling the paradoxes of persuasion, we'll ask you to:

- Lean forward when you want to pull back.
- Make eye contact when you want to look away.
- Ask for more information from someone who is criticizing you.
- Embrace your fear of speaking in public rather than trying to "overcome" it.
- Draw out the shyest or most recalcitrant person in a group.
- Accept a "thank you" without responding, "Oh, it was nothing."

Such behaviors might feel phony—indeed they couldn't feel any other way—to anyone who has spent decades doing the opposite. The good news, though, is that they will not feel phony for long. After several attempts at what feels like "putting on a show," these new actions will begin to feel...merely uncomfortable.

From Discomfort to Second Nature

Why do we say that, after several attempts, the new behaviors would feel "merely uncomfortable"? Because people who are really paying attention to their physical and emotional state as they practice new communication habits will notice a subtle but very significant difference between feeling *phony* and feeling *uncomfortable*. By the time the latter stage is reached, the behaviors will still feel awkward and they won't be easy to perform, but engaging in them won't feel like pretending.

We're aware, of course, that discomfort is rarely presented in a good light. In fact, we noted earlier that 90 percent of health-club rookies dropped out at precisely the stage at which they began to feel physical discomfort (*I'm sore all over*) and emotional discomfort (*this isn't getting me a great body as quickly as I thought it would*). Their distress generates inertia, and their newfound resolve to get in shape at the gym relapses into daily trips to Krispy Kreme.

In our thirty years of teaching effective communication, however, we've observed only about a 20 percent dropout rate in those with whom we've worked. We believe this is because we've prepared them to anticipate and welcome uncomfortable feelings as an indispensable part of habit replacement.

The really encouraging news is that, of those who persist through discomfort and attain the *comfortable* level—the stage where new behaviors still must be thought about but are far easier to undertake—almost all attain the final *natural* level.

At the natural level, new communication habits have fully taken root. No concentration or effort is required. You just do it. This is the stage at which once-novice exercisers factor a workout into their daily routine as a matter of course, the way one might factor in taking a shower or eating lunch. This is the phase at which first-time parents, no longer insecure, know what each of their baby's cries signifies and how to respond. This is when a leader has developed what appears to be an intuitive knack for setting a course and providing motivation.

What onlookers don't know, of course, is that what appears to be intuitive has been carefully and attentively developed over a period of time. This is the kind of "natural" that is more accurately described as "second nature"—an improvement on basic instincts and early learning.

There's a word in Italian, *sprezzatura*, which translates as the ability to take a difficult thing and make it look easy. For us it calls to mind the image of Olympic-level ice skaters, who make their elegant jumps and elaborate turns appear so effortless. *Sprezzatura* is a quality inherent in any endeavor that becomes second nature. To communicate charismatically and persuasively may look easy, but for the vast majority of us it reflects a determined, focused effort and a willingness to tolerate some early unnerving feelings for the sake of a highly rewarding payoff.

Chapter Two

That's Not What I Said…Or Is It?

The Hidden Dimension of Communication

We promised that beginning to change the way you communicate would be unsettling at first. To prove we weren't kidding, we're going to start by saying that oftentimes people are hearing something very different than what we *think* we're saying. Paradoxically, sometimes we're not even communicating what we *firmly believe* we're communicating. That's because communication always has a hidden dimension.

Beam Us Up, Scottie

As any Star Trek fan knows, the universe is full of hidden dimensions. Tripping across one, be it on the far side of a distant nebula or right in your own celestial backyard, is always a tricky business. The unseen is full of cosmic quagmires and subspace sinkholes. Things can go from good to bad, and bad to worse, in a nanosecond. A warp core meltdown is a real possibility.

Communication is much the same: The aspects that are not overt are often the parts that are the most troublesome. When hidden meanings accompany seemingly straightforward content, mixed messages result. We can say one thing while giving others the impression that we are saying the opposite. This is hardly a recipe for building trust or strengthening bonds in any setting.

The hidden dimension of communication actually encompasses a vast realm of material. It includes body language, such as gestures, posture, and facial expressions, and voice mechanics, such as tone, volume, and rate of speech. It also includes word choices, as when someone invokes a figure of speech that can be interpreted in more than one way ("What's good for the goose is good for the gander"), or defaults to a loaded phrase that has historically caused arguments in a relationship ("Here you go again with the whining"). The timing of a communication can also convey hidden meaning. For example, an interruption when someone else is speaking tends to signal, *Nothing you're saying is as important as I am.*

Intent Versus Impact

Human interactions are complicated, and our motives can be quite complex. To set a goal of doing away with hidden communication altogether would be foolhardy. But anyone who aspires to be a truly persuasive communicator must cultivate a new level of awareness that factors in an important reality: *The intent of a message rarely matches its impact.* Let's look at some examples:

> *A manager asks an employee, "Is the report ready yet?"*

> **INTENT:** Where are you in the project?
> **IMPACT:** What's taking you so long?

> *A parent offers to help a high school senior who is filling out a college application.*

INTENT: I can help you edit that.
IMPACT: I don't trust you to do it right.

A husband asks his wife about her mother's forthcoming visit.

INTENT: How long is she staying?
IMPACT: I wish your mother would stay home.

What's going out at one end is not what's being taken in on the other end. In the nanosecond it takes for a message to register with its recipient, there's been a profound shift in meaning. That is because virtually every message spans two levels.

Content Level/Relationship Level

On a content level, every communication in the above examples is meant to contain or request some factual piece of information. A manager seeks details about project status, a parent offers assistance with an application, and a husband requests specifics about his mother-in-law's impending visit. At least, that is what's happening on the surface.

Below the surface, however, deep relationship dynamics are being set in motion. At the relationship level, every message that passes between two parties can be interpreted—or perhaps misinterpreted—as *Here's what I really think.*

Even if we consciously wish to send only pure content, each and every content message gets decoded at a relationship level. In the above cases, the recipients have read the relationship messages as *you're a slacker, you're irresponsible, your mother's a pain.* When the impact of a relationship message is negative, content becomes secondary. Information is held hostage to emotion.

The goal of this chapter is to generate awareness of hidden communication that will help you to put the two levels of messages in synch as frequently as possible. That requires attention to how messages are presented.

The way in which a message is delivered, or packaged, is critical to having it perceived the way we want it to be perceived. Imagine giving a lovely gift of diamond jewelry in a crumpled brown paper bag. Wouldn't it make the person receiving the present wonder if the piece were actually made of cubic zirconium? Imagine offering an expensive perfume in an aluminum can. Do you think the fragrance would appeal? In both cases, the value of something is undermined by an incongruous presentation. As a result, the intent (*here is something luxurious and expensive*) and the impact (*it's probably a cheap fake*) diverge. The same is true for communication. What is sent out is inextricably linked to *how* it's sent.

But I Didn't Mean It That Way

Many times, to be sure, the sender of a message that lands with a "thud" on impact will protest: "But I didn't mean it that way." This usually sets off a volley of "Yes you did" and "No, I didn't" that goes on until one person gives up, exhausted.

A better approach would be for speakers in this situation to consider: *Hey, maybe I really did mean it that way at some level.* It's true that sometimes we're being utterly straightforward, and our meaning is misconstrued. But often, being the complex, multi-faceted creatures that we are, we may have a hidden agenda—an alternate message perhaps so well hidden even from ourselves that, until we examine our communication behavior, we remain unaware.

Poker experts talk about the "tells" that card players unwittingly convey to the watchful observer. These subtle, unconscious giveaways— a shift in one's posture, a lick of the lips, a widening of the eyes—can signal what kind of a hand someone is holding despite that player's conscious intent to be, well, poker-faced.

So, if you do have a hidden agenda, it's worth looking at some of the many ways you may be "telling" about it. By doing so, you can become your own watchful observer, potentially heading off many disconnects between intent and impacts before they ever take place.

How Body Language Broadcasts

Most everyone is familiar with the concept of body language on an intellectual and an intuitive level. We believe, or feel, that when people receive our message with folded arms, crossed legs, and a body that's partially turned away, they're rejecting what we say. When people face us fully, displaying open hands, with feet planted firmly on the ground, we sense that they're accepting our message. We tend to be less conscious, however, of how our own body postures and gestures come across.

Imagine yourself as the manager who asks, "Where are you in the project?" Visualize your foot tapping or your fingertips drumming on a desktop as you pose the question. Your overt intent may be to get a sense of your employee's progress, but your movements telegraph impatience.

Now imagine yourself as a parent saying, "Let me have a look at that application for you." Your aim, so you believe, may be to lovingly offer a helping hand. Now imagine leaning in and moving your hand forward as if to grab the paper as you make that offer. Your teen sees what your bodily eagerness betrays: *You're still a child who can't function without me.*

Finally, see yourself asking your spouse how long your mother-in-law will be visiting. Throw in an eye-roll. Maybe you didn't plan that facial "tell," but at the last second you gave in to emotional impulse. Now you're in the doghouse.

The foot tapping, the hand drumming, the leaning and grabbing, and the eye rolling all telegraph messages that make a powerful impact. The content, ostensibly neutral, takes on a negative charge. Not surprisingly, responses to these "tells" are also negative. The employee is likely to launch into a defense of the project's progress. The teenager is apt to protest the parent's interference or perhaps stalk off sullenly. The wife is apt to provide a laundry list of evidence to the effect that her husband has never liked her mother, never treated her fairly, and never given her a chance (quite possibly followed by a diatribe on how saintly she has been to *his* mother over the years).

In each case, the hidden dimension of communication has triggered an avalanche of bad feeling. Moreover, none of the original content has been addressed productively. If the dialogue continues, intent and impact are apt to diverge even further because, *as the level of conflict rises, so does the potential for distortion.*

If we wish to be persuasive communicators, we must examine our motives and make a serious effort to keep our messages as undistorted as possible. Certainly, we're entitled to have mixed feelings about a situation. But addressing our concerns and airing our doubts directly will go a lot further toward generating trust than will turning mixed feelings into mixed messages.

Managing Micro-Behaviors

Now let's get back to our poker game for a moment. Remember how even the tiniest movements or expressions can be "tells"? So far the kinds of gestures and expressions we've discussed—like foot tapping and eye rolling—aren't exactly subtle. They are blatant macro-behaviors, easy to interpret and, for the aware speaker determined to minimize mixed messages, relatively easy to control. But hidden messages may be revealed even when a speaker's body language consists of almost imperceptible micro-behaviors, as they do in the following example.

At Acme Bank & Trust, new employees are encouraged during their orientation to feel comfortable asking as many questions of their managers as they need to. "Asking questions is a way to shorten your learning curve," they're told in their training. "Your supervisor will welcome questions as signs that you are interested, engaged, and attentive to detail."

But new employee Mike stops asking questions of his supervisor after the first morning on the job. It seems that the first time he asked a question, his boss answered it cheerfully and appropriately enough. However, when he asked for further clarification on two occasions, each answer was preceded with a brief, barely audible sigh—although accompanied by a smile.

Some people are more skilled than others when it comes to reading micro-behaviors and micro-expressions. Although not everyone will decipher each fleeting facial flicker or behavior nuance, most of us can identify, say, a simulated smile, because it doesn't involve the muscles around the eyes as a genuine one does. Mike noticed that his supervisor's smile did not appear altogether natural. He was also sensitive enough to pick up on the sighing, which he interpreted to signify: *Here we go again.*[5]

Not wanting his boss to think him dim-witted, or to lament that valuable time was being wasted on his education, Mike simply gave up. In this instance, communication shut down completely. The supervisor lost a wonderful opportunity to have a lasting, positive influence on a new member of the team.

What could the supervisor have done differently? Were the sighing and the disingenuous smiling even voluntary? Again, think about the poker players. The truth is that subtle, spontaneous behaviors sometimes belie our true feelings *whether we want them to or not.* Caught up in an emotional reaction, the supervisor may well have been unable to control her micro-behaviors and micro-expressions. *Nevertheless, the supervisor was not without means for salvaging an opportunity to communicate.*

If Mike's questions were coming at an inopportune moment, for example, another time could have been set aside to address them. A simple straightforward statement ("It's not a good time right now") would have solved the supervisor's immediate problem, and an alternative solution ("Can we meet before the staff meeting?") would have continued the potential for dialogue.

The Mind's Ear: Decoding Voice Mechanics

The old adage, "It's not what you say but how you say it," is perhaps nowhere more evident than when hidden messages are conveyed by voice mechanics. The tone of our words, how loudly or softly we utter them, and how quickly or slowly we speak all factor in to how a message is perceived.

A sarcastic, frustrated, or resentful tone is rarely lost on anyone. Embellishing the tonal delivery of even one word—even saying someone's name with a harsh inflection—can convey a multitude of information about how agitated, annoyed, or exasperated the speaker is. That's how kids know—simply by hearing their mother or father call out their name in a certain way—when their parents are at the end of their rope. Even dogs understand the tone of their master's voice—that's how they know they're being told they're "bad dogs."

We can all hear in our "mind's ear" the impact an allegedly neutral question—e.g., "Did you take out the trash?"—can have when it's delivered with a high pitch and word accentuation that punches the *you*. The meaning can easily be registered more as "you *are* garbage," rather than as a neutral query about the trashcan's current location.

Making a statement in a voice that's louder or softer than one's usual manner of speaking is another method by which we signal a hidden communication. Loudness often conveys anger, but exaggerated softness can do the same, sometimes in a firmer, more foreboding way. We've all seen movie mobsters threaten those they're about to fit for a pair of cement shoes by practically whispering their malevolent farewell, and the effect can be chilling. Of course a whisper combined with a sweet tone of endearment brings an entirely different context to a message, regardless of its content, which is why we say that lovers like to whisper "sweet nothings" to one another. Sometimes whispering perfectly innocuous information implies that a special secret is being shared and a bond being created.

Our rate of speech—how far apart words are from one another—can also alter the meaning of content. Words delivered at a rapid clip often give the impression the speaker is impatient or intolerant. A slow delivery can imply disinterest or outright boredom.

Combination Packages

In many instances, voice mechanics can combine with body language to convey vivid relationship messages in even the most seemingly simple content. Whenever we address the topic of the richness and ubiquity of relationship messages, we're reminded of a marital communication course we taught when we first arrived at the University of Oregon.

We thought it would be helpful to develop a compendium of fighting issues that plague married couples. We sent out a questionnaire, and in about three months collected more than 300 different fighting issues. To gain additional understanding, we called some of the couples into our office and sat them down face-to-face. We then asked them to reach consensus on what they fought about most. We offer one example of a pattern we observed repeatedly.

Joan, a young mother, said to her husband, "You know, dear, I think we fight most in the morning when we're trying to get the children off to school. I think what we fight most about is who's going to drive them there."

"*No, it isn't!*" replied Harry, her husband. His loud, rapid response, headshake, and wide-eyed expression implied more than disbelief.

The content of the response was simply *I disagree.* But the relationship message as perceived by Joan was, *You're an idiot! How could you be so stupid as to think that's our biggest problem?*

Harry continued in a clipped tone of righteous indignation. "Our main problem happens when we get home in the evening. We fight about who's going to wash the morning dishes, and we fight about who's going to make dinner. Those are our main problems!"

This proved too much for Joan, who crossed her arms and replied with a high-pitched, "What are you talking about? *I* make all the dinners around here! *I'm* the one who's always doing dishes."

This scene repeated itself over and over with different players and different scripts. Married couples would start fighting right in front of us *about what they fought most about!* What became clear very quickly was that the issues themselves were secondary; in fact, they hardly mattered. What did matter was the struggle going on below the surface, at the relationship level of meaning. The specifics of these struggles—*who* felt unfairly treated, *who* felt embittered, *who* felt ignored or misunderstood—were all conveyed on that second level.

Choosing Words Wisely, or Unwisely

A speaker's choice of words can also affect relationship messages. Any number of loaded phrases can tilt the balance of a communication. Some that are especially worth avoiding are those that convey a message about the futility of communication itself. We've yet to come across an instance where it's proved helpful to say:

> *"There you go again."*
>
> *"I heard you the first time."*
>
> *"Where have I heard that before?"*
>
> *"Oh, never mind. Just forget I said anything."*

Some phrases are frequently perceived as an attack on character. Telling someone "you got your way" conveys *the spoiled brat wins again."* Saying "the least you can do" implies *you never do anything*.

Imagine this quick outburst Susan observed at the offices of an insurance company: Carol, an administrative assistant, was feeling stressed beyond her capacity. She spun her revolving chair to face her cubicle partner and implored, "The least you could do when you see me so overwhelmed in here is offer to help, but you NEVER do. All you care about are your own projects."

Martin, her stunned cubicle mate, looked up from his work and replied contemptuously, "Well, if you were more organized and didn't spend so much time on personal phone calls, you wouldn't have to ask me to do your work."

That ended the exchange, but not the bad feelings.

If we asked a random sample of people to tell us what this argument was about, many would say that it was an argument about whether two coworkers should help each other out during heavy workload periods.

Others would say it was about whether help should be expected if the other person isn't doing her share. Carol and Martin didn't focus on either of these content level views. The content was never creatively discussed. Instead, these two people battled it out at the relationship level of meaning. When Carol said, "The least you could do, when you see me so overwhelmed…," the relationship message was, *I can speak to you in any way I want because I have right on my side, and you don't. So when I say jump, you just ask how high.* When Martin answered, "Well, if you were better organized and not wasting so much time on personal phone calls…," he was communicating, *You can't treat me that way, and if you ever talk to me with such disrespect, I'll never do what you ask.* From that moment on, the conversation became nothing more than, *Yes, I can. No, you can't. Yes, I can. No, you can't.* The immediate, practical issues were not addressed—and the work not done.

In this case, both coworkers clearly had axes to grind. Their poor choices of words reflected their hidden agendas, which they were unable or unwilling to raise in more productive ways. Sometimes, however, words chosen in all good faith can create a negative impact because their meaning is unclear. Figures of speech—those little colloquialisms we assume everyone interprets as we do—are notorious culprits in this arena. The following is a good example.

Years ago, while we were facilitating a retreat in Alaska, a conflict broke out between two leaders from different factions of the same group. The interaction was intense as we helped Stella and Dan work out some of their most difficult issues.

We felt grateful about the way the conversation had ended, until Stella said, "Well, I guess we're back to square one."

Dan was stunned, shocked, and angry. When he heard "back to square one," he assumed it meant, *What a waste of time this conversation has been. Nothing has been accomplished. We shouldn't have even had this discussion.*

With further questioning, we discovered Stella's intent was really to say, *We're starting with a clean slate. We have the whole world ahead of us now. This is a new beginning for our relationship.*

The distortion between intent and impact almost shattered an already fragile peace. Fortunately, once we pointed out the mix-up to Stella and Dan, they were able to get past their initial reactions to have a deeper conversation and restore the peace.

Selective Perception

Stella and Dan spoke the same language, yet their dialogue required interpreters. Even though neither one had a hidden agenda, and even though both had an innocent intent, a relationship-level message still managed to register—with a counter-productive impact. In this case, the catalyst was a figure of speech that was interpreted two ways. Remember, the potential for distortion rockets in times of conflict, and Dan and Stella were just wrapping up a difficult negotiation.

Even so, the question arises: Why were both people so eager to seize on a single phrase as proof of irresolution rather than seeking a simple clarification? The answer is that there was yet another hidden dimension factor at work.

That factor is something known as *selective perception*. Selective perception has to do with expectations. In our day-to-day lives, we function efficiently by navigating our way through the familiar. We expect things to be as we left them, and that expectation influences our behaviors. When we're at home, for example, we can walk into our kitchen, even half asleep, and know how to make a cup of coffee and feed the cat. We don't have to give these matters our complete attention; we're on automatic pilot.

We are often selectively perceptive about people, too. Have you ever had an experience where someone you know shaves his mustache or dyes her hair, and you are so oblivious to the change that they end up asking you, "Don't you notice anything different about me?" Now suppose that person has changed his or her attitude instead of appearance?

Imagine how long it might take you to notice. If you expect people to be, say, contentious, you may block out any indication that they're now agreeable.

No one is consistently one way all of the time. Though people have tendencies to act and think in a particular fashion, the "self" is not a concept set in stone. Even the most ornery curmudgeon may at times act out of compassion; even the most selfish have flashes of generosity. Have you ever heard a renowned sourpuss make a really funny, self-deprecating remark? Renowned sourpusses sometimes do—but perhaps you didn't notice.

Now think about your own dominant personality traits, the ones you display much of the time. Are there times when you are feeling differently, acting differently, operating—so to speak—outside your box? Of course there are, but no matter how sincerely you are showing another side of yourself, this may not always register with others, because they are still looking for—and probably finding—the parts of you they expect to see.

It's not our nature to anticipate exceptions to what we think are the rules in our relationships. Instead, we consistently review the behavior of others, picking and choosing examples that confirm our theory of what they're like. Then we tell ourselves, "I knew it!" If we treat people as we expect them to be—rather than pay attention to how they are right now—we will fail to persuade.

We observed an interesting example of selective perception when, as consultants to a school system, we were called into a particular high school to smooth out issues between faculty and staff. Virtually everyone we interviewed said: "If you want to know the problem in this school, it's the principal. She's insulting. She insults us in front of students, in front of each other, even in front of parents."

We asked for examples. "Oh, that's easy," said one of the teachers. "Just ten minutes ago, I was standing by the copy machine, minding my own business, and she walked over to me and said, 'My, you look nice today.'"

Confused, we asked, "Then what happened?"

The teacher explained, "Don't you get it? 'My, you look nice today.' She was trying to tell me I look awful every other day."

This teacher was so invested in experiencing the principal as insulting that even a compliment was taken as an affront.

The As-If Principle

Reading this story as an outsider, an observer, it's easy to say, "Wow, that's ridiculous." But the truth is that, in most situations in our personal and professional lives, all of us see each other through the distorted, foggy filters of expectation.

Then things get even more complicated. Once we're emotionally invested in our distorted perceptions, we act "as if" people will behave a certain way. And indeed they begin to play out the role that we have assigned to them.

In a famous study known as "Pygmalion in the Classroom," psychologists Robert Rosenthal and Lenore Jacobsen proved the astonishing power of such self-fulfilling prophecies. The two researchers, who had spent much of their careers in education, conducted an experiment in which teachers were told that certain elementary-level students—actually randomly selected—had been identified by a special test as "academic spurters" who would make rapid and impressive intellectual progress in the coming school year.[6] This created expectations in teachers who were assigned to work with the "special" group. Over the next eight months, the "spurters" were subjectively rated as better behaved, more intellectually curious, friendlier, and more likely to achieve future success than their "ordinary" counterparts.

Now comes the truly frightening part: When students took IQ tests at the school year's end, there was significantly higher scoring in the "spurter" group. Clearly, the teachers' expectations of the students affected the students' expectations of themselves and, by extension, their actual performance.

That is a breathtaking example of the "as-if" principle in action. And in the years since this original 1968 experiment, there have been many more. Researchers have examined interpersonal expectancy effects in a variety of contexts. Their studies have demonstrated, among other things, that leaders' expectations have an impact on organizational effectiveness, that juries are more likely to give guilty verdicts when the trial judge expects defendants to be guilty, and that depression among nursing home patients can be decreased by raising the expectations of their caregivers.

Shifting the System

Whenever we're interacting with others, we are part of a communication system. Like a complex construction of gears, levers, and pulleys, when one part of the system moves, the other elements move to accommodate it. Thus, if someone is feeling negatively toward you, the impact of your messages may be anticipated as negative. Worse, before you know it, you may actually accommodate that expectation by turning negative—even if that was not your original intent.

Is that fair? Well, no. Is it a fact? Alas, yes.

But here's one of the paradoxes of persuasion: While it is true that you cannot control someone else's thought process or behavior, you can certainly alter your own thoughts and actions. Remember, all it takes to change a system is an alteration in one part. As demonstrated in Leader Insight 2-1 on page 44, persuasive communicators can take responsibility for shifting a communication system by:

- Acknowledging that they speak at both content and relationship levels simultaneously.
- Aligning body language, voice mechanics, and word choices with intended messages as much as possible so that intent does not diverge from impact.

- Acknowledging any mixed feelings, should they exist, and raising issues and concerns straightforwardly.
- Remaining conscious of the temptation to assign and play out assigned roles "as if" they were real.

Leader Insight 2-1

When Diplomacy Requires Countering Expectations

Charles "Butch" Swindells, American Ambassador to New Zealand, has many pleasant duties but also many difficult aspects to his job. He has been attempting to get New Zealand to rethink its "nuclear free zone" policy, which prevents American nuclear-propelled ships from entering its waters. He must also interact frequently with New Zealanders who oppose U.S. foreign policies.

"As a representative for the world's only super power, the expectation is that I'll be a bully," says Swindells. "I need to prove that I'm not." To counter negative assumptions, Swindells is determined to stay "passionate, optimistic, and accessible."

He says, "On one tour of the country, I was addressing 250 people in a town of 1200—a farming community in the central South Island, called Timaru. There were ministers and others so angry about the U.S. war action in Iraq. I told them, 'I'm not here to persuade you to accept our thought process, but to dialogue with you.' Then at the end of the meeting, I spoke directly to my greatest critic in the audience. 'I appreciate your feelings, I know I haven't persuaded you. I thank you for letting me talk.'"

Understanding as Empowerment

It's often all too easy to get caught up in the dynamics of a communication system. These dynamics can sometimes unfold so quickly, and with so much emotional momentum, that they are difficult to counter. This is especially true when there is conflict in a relationship.

In this challenge, awareness is the persuasive communicator's most effective tool. Keeping the hidden dimension of communication in mind is empowering. It allows us to more clearly comprehend and affect the full force of what we say at all levels. As you use the models presented in this book, you will begin to master the paradoxes of persuasion as you take control of your impact and your influence.

Chapter Three

Is That What Really Happened?
The Perception-Reality Gap

In the previous chapter, we saw that people experience what they *expect* to experience when they interact with someone else. We saw that expectations are so powerful, so ingrained, that they can easily distort the way reality is perceived.

For most of us, it's relatively easy to think of times when we've been misunderstood because we're on the receiving end of perceptual distortions. We'd wager that if we were to ask anyone reading this book if people ever made erroneous judgments about them based on false assumptions, they would quickly come up with numerous examples.

It's a less simple matter, however, to recall instances where we've been the ones *making* incorrect assumptions. Most of us assume that our perceptions about people and events are usually correct. Well, that itself is a *false assumption*.

Most of us misperceive behavior and situations far more often than we'd care to admit. It's not unusual for our "take" on an interaction to be wrong. All of us have certain gaps between what we perceive to be happening and what's actually going on.

No one is immune to this perception-reality gap—not even those who study it professionally. To illustrate, we'll tell you about an event that occurred when the two of us were conducting a leadership communication seminar for a large corporate group.

While most of the audience members seemed to be alert and engaged, one particular woman looked vexed, perplexed, and utterly discombobulated. She stared at us with squinted eyes, slackened her jaw, hunched her shoulders and tilted her head pronouncedly to one side.

It's a natural tendency for the human mind to focus on perceived threats to equanimity—and so both of us honed in on this lady and went through a series of mental contortions of our own. *Why was she looking at us as if we had just dropped in from Jupiter? Were our clothes on inside out? Were we saying something unclear, obtuse, insensitive? Should we change what we were doing: speed up, slow down, give up altogether?*

Ultimately, we exchanged helpless glances with one another and forged ahead, trying as hard as we could to focus on anything but this seemingly confounded participant who had suddenly come to embody for us the distinct possibility that we were *utter frauds and complete failures*.

Imagine our surprise when the session was over and this woman stayed behind and approached us, saying, "Wow, what a wonderful presentation. I was bowled over. It was so easy to understand. I can't wait to put these principles into action. I can think of three or four relationships these skills can help me repair."

We exchanged glances again. Clearly, this was a moment to employ one of the principles that breaks through the paradoxes of persuasion: *Perceptions require reality checks.*

Susan turned to our seminar participant and said, "I'm so glad you came up to talk. I'm a little confused about something. Maybe you can help me clear it up. When I looked at you in the audience, I noticed you were leaning forward and squinting. I was thinking that maybe some of our material was confusing to you or that it seemed off the mark. Where did I go wrong?"

"Oh, no," said the woman. "No, everything you said was crystal clear. But I just got these new trifocals today and I can't figure out how to look through the middle lens. The eye doctor said it would take a while to get used to them, but they're really annoying."

Oh! The three of us broke out laughing. We had just spontaneously created evidence of one of our key points. We're all so used to jumping to conclusions, and once we "conclude" something, that's usually the end of the story. But another person's reality is often a different matter altogether.

A Model for Perception Checking

How Susan got to the reality of the seminar participant, quickly and effectively cutting off a misunderstanding that might have lingered indefinitely, may, at first glance, look like a spontaneous communication. Naturally, there was some spontaneity involved, since Susan was dealing with particular circumstances that arose from the situation. But what Susan said was based on a model—a communication method designed specifically for checking perceptions against reality.

Perception checking is a method that involves describing the specific behaviors that you perceive as well as the interpretations that you are making about those behaviors. The model can be adapted to virtually any circumstances. Its structure would remain the same, though specific details would, of course, vary.

Here's how the model would work in a situation where communication has stopped between coworkers after one of them moved from a cubicle into an office:

> **Opener**—Obtain tacit approval for a perception check: "I'd like to check something out with you if that's all right," or "I'm not sure I'm reading events correctly. Can you help me out?"

Note behaviors you observe—Share specifics about events and behavior that have made an impression on you. In this instance: "I've noticed you haven't been talking to me, and your silence seems to coincide with my moving into my new office."

State your assumption—Be sure to phrase your query about what's going on as a supposition, not a fact. In this example: "I'm not sure, but it seems like you might feel I'm getting preferential treatment." *It's critical that these assumptions be phrased tentatively. Remember, so far they are only your interpretations—not facts!*

Ask for confirmation—Seek corroboration, again phrasing your words tentatively: "Am I reading things accurately?"

Any of a number of responses might be elicited by the person checking perceptions. The coworker might admit to feeling resentful, or voice an objection to being left in a cubicle while someone else was allotted four walls and a door. Yet that would be a positive outcome because it would pave the way for a sensitive issue to be addressed in a forthright way.

The coworker might also say, "Oh no, I've just been busy." That might seem like a dismissal of the problem, but the perception checker has at least cracked open the door to communication, and can reinforce that opening by saying, "Okay. Well, please let me know if there's anything you think we should discuss about this."

Remember, our perceptions are wrong 50 percent of the time. That means there's a fair shot that the coworker might surprise the perception checker by saying something one hundred and eighty degrees from what was anticipated, such as, "Gosh, I'm glad you brought this up. I feel like we never get to chat anymore since you moved to that office. I miss talking to you."

As with all of these new communication behaviors, perception checking will feel alien to you when you first give it a go. We're not used to describing specific behaviors we observe, and first attempts can be awkward. We may fear giving offense, but bear in mind that the best way to avoid giving offense is to keep those descriptions very neutral and objective. It's one thing to say, "You haven't been talking to me"; it's quite another to say, "You've been ignoring me." The latter statement—which uses the pejorative word *ignore* and insinuates negative intent—is bound to put someone on the defensive.

Another thing we may fear about perception checking is what we're going to find out. Maybe we're right, *but do we really want to know?* Maybe we're wrong—and if so, do we want to know *that?* The truth is, however, that the more you value a relationship, the more you owe it to yourself, to the other person, and to the relationship itself to hold your version of reality up to the light and examine it thoroughly. To respect someone means giving that person a chance to understand—and respond to—your perception of events.

When Perceptions Go Unchecked

Despite initial resistance to perception checking, once people get used to implementing this skill, they tend to relish their newfound ability. In fact, in one of our research studies, people reported back to us that this was the new communication model they used more than any other. What they appreciated most about mastering it was that perception checking has the power to interrupt very negative communication cycles that might otherwise spiral out of control.

Let's take a look at the typical way in which our perceptions generate thoughts, feelings, desires, and actions.[7] [see Figure 3-A on page 52] In the preceding example, one employee (Tom) noticed that his co-worker (Joan) was no longer speaking to him. If Tom hadn't used perception checking, his internal emotional process might well have unfolded like this:

Hmmm, I SEE that Joan hasn't been speaking to me since
I got my new office. I THINK she is jealous, and now
she doesn't want to be my friend anymore. I FEEL angry,
really betrayed. Joan is supposed to be happy for me. I
WANT to show her this doesn't bother me, though. I

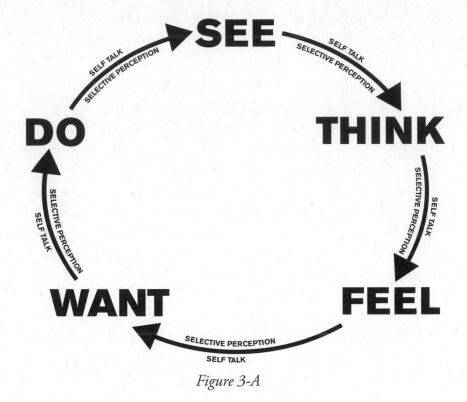

Figure 3-A

know what I'll DO. I'm going to ignore *her*. If I have to tell her something, I'll send her an email—a nasty email. I'll show her she can't do this to me.

It's all too easy to see how this kind of inner dialogue can evolve, and how most of us can be emotionally seduced by this type of negative progression. But note one very important thing: Tom actually did SEE a behavior. He didn't imagine the fact that Joan wasn't speaking to him. Joan's silence was a verifiable fact. However, from that initial perception onward, everything else that had emotional resonance for Tom was merely self-talk.

With self-talk as our only reference point, we can whip ourselves into a frenzy based solely on our own unchecked interpretation of a situation. We think we know what a behavior means: *Joan doesn't want to be my friend.*

That subjective thought generates intense feeling: *Poor me!*

That feeling in turn creates desires inside of us, and we carry out actions to fulfill those desires: *I'll do whatever I have to do to get even.*

Now ponder for a moment the potential for this dynamic to spread harm.

What might well have happened next in Tom and Joan's case was nothing less than a factionalization of the entire office. Tom might have shared his perception that Joan was petty and envious with several of his coworkers. Joan might have circulated Tom's ungracious email. Soon the entire office would be put in a position of choosing sides and acting out their allegiances by thwarting the other group. All of this because one perception went unverified.

Leader Insight 3-1

People and Money: Always a Delicate Issue

Issues of money are always delicate issues. If not properly addressed, they can create an enormous amount of antagonism. The best way to resolve such matters is to face them head on, as did Mike Long, a senior-level manager for the Oregon Department of Transportation (O.D.O.T.).

O.D.O.T. was in the midst of a major, ongoing reorganization, and a part of Mike's division's budget was reallocated to another division. "My understanding was that I would continue to administer those funds from my sector," Long explained. "But I learned that a new manager assumed otherwise."

Long called a meeting with the head of the other department and his senior staff. "Before the meeting," Long said, "I determined what their main concerns were, and how I might address them but continue to administer the funds from my area.

"I took responsibility for the miscommunication," Long said. "I then explained that this particular piece of my budget was integrated with another piece, and I gave clear-cut examples of how this integration worked. Without the two budgets connected, progress we'd made in project delivery would be diminished. I also agreed to have this other department participate in the fieldwork for the projects in question and so receive part of the funding—though not administer it. That seemed to satisfy everybody."

The meeting ended with a written agreement. Even more important was the long-term result. The two departments established a level of trust and a solid working relationship, which they could rely on to solve future problems together.

Leader Insight 3-2

Bringing Communication Out of the Darkness Into the Light

At the MacLaren Youth Correctional Facility, one of the largest in the Northwest, staff members are required to be on duty 24/7. Many who work the graveyard shift rarely see their coworkers—but communication takes place between them nonetheless. Sometimes, says superintendent Gary Lawhead, the main source of that communication can be the grapevine. "Grapevine communication can create rumors with large perception errors," says Lawhead. "Rumors are prone to overstatement. They often contain words like 'always' and 'never.'"

One of Lawhead's communication challenges, he says, is to make certain that everyone gets the same information. This became critical when a project was conceived to fence the 95-acre facility. "This facility had stood for 75 years without a fence surrounding it," he explained. "People were used to things the way they were. For example, many employees who used to drive directly to the building would now be required to park much further away and walk a good distance."

Because the fence would provide many advantages to the facility and the community surrounding it, Lawhead decided to bring all of the stakeholders together.

"When we see perceptions are not accurate, we get people together and try to sort through them," he said. "What we did in preparation for the fence project was to have a representative from each group—schooling, security, food service, and so on—be part of an ongoing work group. We also invited the mayor of the town and chief of police to participate in these groups with us.

"What came out of this dynamic," Lawhead continued, "was that the mayor and the chief were able to give the discussion a kick start and put things in perspective. It was better than my saying, 'Here's the change, get over it.' Often, group members say things that I as a leader cannot say. This is a far better model than the grapevine when it comes to getting people to understand and accept a change. With grapevine communication, a small group of unhappy people passes around negative information. When you shed light on the information, you connect with the silent majority and with the people who have good ideas and are willing to be vocally positive."

Retrieving Relationships with Perception Checking

Leader Insights 3-1 and 3-2 demonstrate how perception checking can be used proactively to head off negative spirals before they begin. It can also be used retroactively. Many of our alumni tell us they have used their perception-checking skill to help retrieve relationships that had fallen away for reasons that were never discussed outright.

Many of us have had the experience of falling out of touch with a friend or loved one after some unsettling but minor misunderstanding. The following is a story from one of our former workshop participants, Barbara. Barbara finally got to the bottom of such a situation by checking her initial interpretation of what went on. Here's what happened:

Last year, on the Fourth of July, Barbara had a friend from the city out to her country house for the day. The friend brought along her dog, a full-grown standard poodle she'd recently adopted, and was excited to give her new pet a day outdoors. Barbara's family has a dog as well—a male golden retriever named Bo.

Nobody was concerned about the possibility that the dogs might not get along. Bo was a gentle soul, and Barbara's friend's dog, Luna, was reputed to be the same. When the canines met, though, there was a bit of a problem. Bo seemed to feel romantically inclined towards the poodle, and eager to display his affections in the way dogs do. Luna seemed uninterested in returning his affections.

While Barbara and her husband thought this all rather harmless—after all, Luna was spayed—their friend took umbrage at Bo's amorous advances, insisting they separate the dogs, both of whom then started whining and barking. For all the humans, it was a fairly miserable Fourth of July. Barbara's friend was anxious about her dog. She was so clearly stressed out that at one point Barbara even offered her a mild tranquilizer. The friend declined and instead left early.

Months went by and Barbara never heard from her friend. The friend never wrote or called to say thank you, as was her custom. She never called or sent a card for Barbara's birthday. When the holidays came and went without even a card, Barbara decided to call her friend. She was prepared to do a perception check on the situation—which, at the time, meant she was ready to confirm her perception that her friend was still angry about the way Bo behaved. Even though Barbara was a little annoyed and thought her friend silly for holding this grudge—dogs will be dogs—she thought she could persuade her friend to put this all behind them.

When Barbara got her friend on the phone, she told her she'd missed being in touch. She said, "'I'm guessing you're not contacting me because you're still upset about how Bo behaved."

"Oh, no," her friend said, "Dogs will be dogs. I'm upset because you offered me a tranquilizer. When you did that, I thought you were trying to tell me I was crazy."

Barbara was flabbergasted. It had never occurred to her that she had offended her friend in this way. Barbara apologized, and assured her friend it was certainly not her intention to communicate that she was "crazy." Now Barbara could see how things had gone from bad to worse because none of this had ever come out in the open.

Barbara's perception-checking conversation had gone in a completely different direction than she'd anticipated, but the outcome was what she'd hoped for: the friendship was restored.

It took courage for Barbara to communicate in this way. After all, she could easily have made a choice to simply wait and hope that the problem—whatever it was—would blow over. It's often more comfortable to remain in our own private bubble and leave our version of events unchallenged. Sure, we may be cut off from others, but at least we don't risk having our take on reality upset.

Yet, combining courage with communication skill can be both preventive medicine and a healing practice. Perception checking is very powerful when employed early, but it is rarely too late to use it. Even long-lingering negative situations can be cleared up more easily than most of us imagine.

Of course, we don't want to leave you with the impression that every situation where perception checking is used will end "happily ever after." There's always a chance you might unearth a reality that you're not thrilled to discover.

Will someone criticize your behavior? Perhaps.

Will a conflict ensue? Possibly.

But that doesn't mean you ought to bury your head in the sand. As the next chapter explains, it's impossible to untangle the paradoxes of persuasion and be a truly influential communicator without embracing criticism and conflict.

Chapter Four

Good News and Bad:
Courting Conflict and Criticism

People don't like criticism. We don't care if it's so-called constructive criticism, if it's sugar coated, or if it's dipped in Belgian chocolate and delivered with a dozen roses.

Many of us do everything in our power to avoid exposing ourselves to criticism. We willfully steer clear of people who might offer negative feedback and of situations where such feedback might create a conflict. When we can't avoid criticism, we experience a visceral physical reaction toward any speaker who is enumerating our wrongs. We tighten up and pull away. We fold our arms defensively across our chest. Some of us may feel flushed in the face; others may have butterflies in the stomach. From the first critical word we hear, our minds get busy mounting an internal counter-offensive that we just can't wait to unleash.

Oh, yeah? we think. *You say I've got a problem. Let me tell you something, buddy. You're the one who blah blah blah. And what about the time you yadda yadda ya? And that's not to mention....*

Okay, maybe some among us who consider ourselves truly evolved will reply to criticism with a taut, "Thank you for sharing." But after our disingenuous conversation is over, we immediately think to ourselves: *Yeah, right. You haven't heard the last from me!*

As longtime researchers in the field of communication and conflict resolution, we acknowledge that all of these responses are perfectly natural, instinctive reactions to criticism. We default to a defensive mode because our bodies and minds perceive criticism as a threat to be defended against. Physiologically, we react to criticism the same way our ancestors reacted to, say, a saber-toothed tiger. Our flight-or-fight response takes over.

But in a complex, interactive civilization, going with one's primal instincts is not always—or indeed often—a winning strategy. Here's a paradox: The consequences of battling or deflecting criticism are far worse than experiencing the initial discomfort of learning to cope with it and, indeed, to welcome it.

In this chapter we're going to provide you with a model for changing the way you respond to criticism—physically, mentally, emotionally, and verbally. Basically, we're going to help you to be quiet and hear the words you need to hear. As you begin to use this model, you will improve the quality of your professional performance and affiliations and enhance the relationships in your private life.

First, though, let's have a look at what happens when criticism and conflict are willfully avoided.

Criticism Always Goes Somewhere

In many organizations, top decision-makers are out of the loop with regard to problems, concerns, or complaints. The reason: negative feedback that's been generated in the ranks has either *not* traveled up the chain of command, or has arrived at the eleventh hour and then been largely ignored. This common communication phenomenon plays an enormous role in organizational dysfunction—because leaders can't make sound decisions when they're uninformed. Not surprisingly, this resistance to forwarding negative news is credited with playing a significant role in a number of infamous and tragic events—Bay of the Pigs, both Challenger and Columbia space shuttle catastrophes, and even 9/11. Radically different measures might well have been taken had a fair hearing been given to the dire warnings of people with firsthand knowledge of problems.

Consider how the systemic suppression of criticism contributed to NASA's Challenger disaster. According to investigations carried out in the aftermath of the incident, a tendency for the now notorious "O" rings to malfunction at low temperatures had been noted by engineers well before the explosion of January 28, 1986. Many credit the tragic decision to the circumstances surrounding the launch—notably the intense media attention attracted by the teacher-in-space program, pressure from Washington, and the repeated delays that had already occurred. But a thirteen-member presidential commission blamed NASA for faulty decision-making. Why did such a decision have to be made under pressure if the potential for failure was already known? The reason lies in a culture with the habit of ignoring negative news. After all, went this particular rationale, if you listened to engineers, who always want more data and consistently err on the side of caution, you'd never get anything done.

After the Challenger, steps were allegedly put into place to avoid similar dynamics and similar disasters. But old cultures die hard, and complacency is tenacious. Years later, not enough attention was paid when concerns were voiced about vulnerabilities of the shuttle Columbia due to damage to its heat-resistant tiles. Columbia's skin was almost certainly compromised, allowing superheated air to enter its left wing during descent.

This avoidance dynamic is hardly limited to the world of government organizations and large corporations. It duplicates itself in small businesses, in social groups, and in family systems. In families, a "don't criticize so-and-so" rule is often in place. Even if the rule is unspoken, everyone silently conspires to abide by it.

Family members don't dare tell Dad that they think he's too tight with money or Grandma that she has a tendency to meddle. Or, we should say, no one tells them to their face. What family members do instead is complain to one another, over and over. They start actively looking for evidence to confirm their criticism, and then eagerly share anecdotes that prove their points:

Dad won't pay for cable, so we just get three TV channels. He's a cheap-skate.

Grandma's always asking the kids when they're going to get married. She can't mind her own business.

Dad and Grandma don't get a chance to explain their perspective, and they certainly don't gain any incentive for changing their behavior. The cycle self-perpetuates and everything stays the same.

Creating Self-Fulfilling Prophecies

It's not hard to understand why most people are all too ready to buy into an edict that says, "Don't criticize people to their face." Would-be critics fear unhappy consequences, and their fears are well founded. If we don't choose flight, we often get a fight.

Here's an example: Pam walks into Laura's office cubicle and says, "Listen, Laura, I can't hear myself think when you're talking on the phone. Can't you lower your voice?"

Laura's response is to immediately criticize the criticizer. "Hey, when I'm talking on the phone it's because I 'm getting some work done. Why don't you try it?"

Pam retaliates, and with each volley the ante tends to be raised. "Getting work done? Were you getting work done when you were talking to your mother this morning?"

"My mother is eighty-three years old and hard of hearing. Thanks for your compassion."

Now we have a full-blown conflict. Alas, it's not the kind of conflict that generates resolution but the kind in which no one's behavior alters, except perhaps for the worse. Do you think anything about this exchange will inspire Laura to lower her voice or Pam to show more compassion?

Remember the "as-if" principle: When we expect someone to behave a certain way, they often fulfill our prophecy. Here's another paradox: Our natural tendency in conflict is to draw out from one another the worst possible behaviors. These are the ones we tell ourselves we least wish to see, but they are also the ones that gratify us on some level by confirming that we were right all along.

Have you ever criticized someone for being short-tempered only to watch him fly off the handle? Have you ever criticized someone for being uncommunicative only to watch her shut down completely? Sure, you get the momentary satisfaction of having proved your point to yourself. But you haven't proved a thing to them. The person you've criticized is now in the "I'll show you" mode.

Thriving on Criticism

The end result of defending against criticism—without *listening* to it—is often a stalemate where no resolution is achieved. Aristotle might say you are the fool persuading only yourself. In such a situation, byproducts include tension (Pam and Laura *really* tighten up when they see each other now), factionalization (each tells her side of the story and seeks allies), and decreased cooperation (the parties can't work together in any productive way).

But what if resolution could be achieved?

Breakthroughs occur when criticism is truly heard and the positive potential of conflict is fully appreciated. Instead of dreading criticism and conflict, we must recognize them for what they are—*opportunities for generating creative solutions to problems, for gaining new perspectives, and for enhancing personal and professional relationships.*

We said earlier that changing our attitude about criticism would mean acknowledging a paradox and acting counter-intuitively. We also said it would take time. Of course, we've got to start somewhere, so the question is: Where do we begin?

If you think about it, there can only be one answer to such a question. Each of us can only start with our self. None of us can wave a wand

and get someone else to change. However, every one of us has the power to change our own behavior. In so doing, we generate a subtle but irrevocable shift in the communication system. Once the system shifts, other people in it alter their reactions as an adaptation to new circumstances. In this way, one "unnatural act" of responding to criticism *by inviting it in* breeds an organic evolution of positive events. The examples in Leader Insights 4-1 and 4-2 demonstrate the positive effects of inviting criticism.

Leader Insight 4-1

All Behavior is Rational to the Behavor

Cheryl Miller, Chief Executive of East Sussex County Council, England, says: "It doesn't matter how obstinate, irrational, or prejudiced another person's opinion. Until you accept that, to them, it's a good and rational reason, you will never understand the 'why'—and will never resolve the problem. I have no difficulty admitting my personal vulnerability—admitting what I don't know and can't do. This is what opens up other people to acknowledge their own vulnerability and fallibility."

Leader Insight 4-2

Senior Managers Solicit and Respond to Criticism

In 1997, Intel Corporation—the world's largest chip maker and a leading manufacturer of computer, networking, and communications products—made a major change in the way it measured the performance of senior-level site managers of its plants around the globe. "Instead of measuring performance based on the output of product or the cost of output," explained CEO David Marsing, "the site managers, each of whom was responsible for their region, would now be evaluated on three communication-based components."

The first performance measure involved Intel's relationship with the external local community. Site managers were required to distribute a survey and talk to community leaders in order to understand the plant's impact on the population. "We wanted to know the impact of having our operation in that region," said Marsing, "and to learn whether we were meeting the community's expectations." (As part of this component, managers were required to put together a five-year action plan, which included a minimum of two meetings per year with a community advisory panel that provided ongoing feedback.)

"The second dimension," said Marsing, "involved conducting a culture survey—assessing the morale of the workforce and defining the issues that existed in the workplace. The real yardstick was ongoing communication with employees, meeting with them and getting live feedback." Once again, an action plan was required, and ongoing performance was evaluated on progress made.

The third component of Marsing's cultural performance measurement called for external and internal customer surveys. Feedback was solicited from anyone who depended on the site managers' work. Another action plan was called for, requiring managers to map out what they would do to improve their level, quality, and cost of service. "The managers were encouraged to get at the source of any problem and talk to the customer involved," Marsing explained. "We wanted them to find out what the real issue was and communicate about it."

"It's all about communication," Marsing said, as he summed up the philosophy behind the new performance-management criteria. "We looked at relationships—with the community, with customers, with downstream employees."

How did the new measurement metrics work out? "The first year was very tough," said Marsing. "Our people felt like they were 'failing.' We kept saying, 'This is really good feedback and it doesn't mean you're failing. It just means you have not been paying attention to some things.'

"All of the managers experienced a similar phenomenon regarding the community-relationship aspect," Marsing added. "Here was a situation where they had no authority and were getting very direct feedback. They had to receive very critical feedback and not respond in 'alpha male' mode." Marsing noted, "The people who identified the issues and went after them in a very systematic way tended to have very consistent performance: both lower costs and higher yields."

A Model for Responding to Criticism

Our model for responding to criticism is one we've provided to hundreds of thousands of people across the globe. Our published follow-up studies and informal feedback have convinced us that a great many of these people have used the model consistently and have realized significant improvements in their personal and professional relationships.

The Responding to Criticism model has two main stages. The first is "Get More Information." We know, we know—hearing something negative about yourself is bad enough. Why would you want *more* information on the topic? Because more information is needed in order to carry out the critical second stage: "Seek out Agreement." Seeds of agreement, no matter how tiny or how dormant, lie within every disagreement. It takes close examination to identify them, and getting more information is the best way to begin.

In overview form, the Responding to Criticism model looks like this: [see Figure 4-A on page 68]

Step 1: Active Listening

The Get More Information stage begins with the seemingly simple act of listening. Some people are good listeners. Under ordinary circumstances they listen actively, with genuine engagement and curiosity. Their interest is manifested in their body language and their spoken reactions. But very few of us are capable of listening in such a manner when we're being criticized.

Remember, we instinctively interpret criticism as a threat. As a result, our bodily reaction is to back away from the critic. In order to further tune out the speaker, we may avoid eye contact, cross our arms, and assume a blank facial expression. Such a rigid, disengaged posture actually makes it more difficult to process information. Speakers and listeners become frustrated, and messages waft, unheeded, into the stratosphere.

Alternatively, we can assume a posture of curiosity. Counter-intuitive though it may be, behave as though the speaker is telling you something you find objectively fascinating. Lean in, keep your arms unfolded, nod when you understand, and maintain all-important eye contact. This posture serves two functions:

- It signals to critics that they're being heard, so they feel less defensive.
- It helps the listener to understand and process what's being said.

Remember, we're in the stage of getting more information so we can seek out agreement. We want to encourage the critic to deliver the message, and we want to understand it.

But what about our verbal reactions? In ordinary discourse we offer sounds or phrases of encouragement ("mmm hmmm, I see...") to indicate our understanding and to keep a speaker going. Not so when we're being criticized. When we're being criticized, we don't *want* to encourage

A Model for Responding
to Criticism—Summary

I. Get more information

Active Listening—Nonverbal curiosity and paraphrasing

Nonverbal Attention—A posture of curiosity

Paraphrasing—Listening to the message, reflecting it back; discovering speaker's intent

STEP 2

Ask for Details—Request clarifying information

STEP 3

Guess—When a speaker can't think of a specific, you come up with one

II. Agreement—Seek out agreement, wherever it exists

Agree with Facts—Be explicit in your agreement

Agree with Critic's Perception—Acknowledge the critic's perception is reasonable

Figure 4-A

the speaker. Besides, we're too busy crafting a rebuttal to devote much energy to those little verbal prods. Instead of clamming up or planning retorts, however, we advise paraphrasing the critic's messages.

The Promise—and Pitfalls—of Paraphrasing

Simply defined, paraphrasing means listening to a message and reflecting it back—restating the speaker's content, intent, and feelings. Paraphrasing improves listening and helps us get more information:

- It allows the listener to clarify confusing information.
- It allows critics to feel they're really being heard.
- It helps the listener to defuse negative emotions.
- It allows the listener to summarize the critic's needs.
- It enables the listener to buy time while figuring out what else to say.

But, wait! We know lots of people have probably heard of this technique. In our workshops many participants even say they've tried it, with mixed results. The skill of paraphrasing is easy to misunderstand and to execute poorly. Let's review and clarify this skill, even for those who think they've "got it."

Paraphrasing is a means for discovering and communicating the speaker's intent. Remember, intent is what the speaker is trying to accomplish with the message; this intent may be quite different than the actual impact of the message. Let's take this message from wife to husband as an example:

> **She:** *"I never know when to start dinner because you never call to tell me when you'll be home. It's infuriating."*

Here, the intent of the wife is (a) to convey frustration and (b) to get her husband to change his behavior by calling ahead. An ineffective execution of reflecting back the critic's intention might go like this:

> **He:** *"So what I hear you saying is…you're angry."*
> **She:** *"I just said that. How do you expect me to plan my day around*

your schedule when I never know what your schedule is? Am I psy-chic?"

He: *"So what I hear you saying is, you're not psychic."*

She: *"If I was psychic I'd know why you're such a jerk."*

He: *"So what I hear you saying is…I'm a jerk!"*

What's wrong with this picture? For one thing, the responder is us-ing the same introductory phrase each time. This smacks of "technique speak," and comes off as insincere and trite, even if well intentioned. Also, the listener isn't attempting to discover what the speaker wants, but merely parroting phrases almost word for word. This adds nothing to the dialogue and can actually escalate a situation. Having "jerk" said aloud two times is twice as provocative as having it said once.

A more effective version of this scenario could go as follows:

She: *"I never know when to start dinner because you never call to tell me when you'll be home. It's infuriating."*

He: *"Wow. So here you put in an incredible effort to make us din-ner, and then you end up frustrated and upset."*

She: *"How do you expect me to plan my day around your schedule when I never know what your schedule is? Am I psychic?"*

He: *"A person would have to be a mind reader to figure that out."*

She: *"That's right."*

He: *"So, it would be much better for you if I'd call as soon as I know what time I'll be leaving work."*

She: *"Right."*

Another way to miss the boat when paraphrasing is to undershoot the emotional intensity of the speaker. Every communication has a cer-tain amount of emotional energy attached to it. Effective paraphrasing matches that level. If we undershoot the emotion, our response can seem flippant and dismissive:

He: *"You completely trivialized my ideas in that meeting. You made me look like an idiot in front of everyone!'"*

She: *"I see you're kind of annoyed with me."*

Now the speaker is left feeling not only misunderstood but also victimized by a power differential. The first party has obviously invested much more in this communication than the second party is willing to. A better response might have been, "So, you're really feeling like I completely dismissed you at the meeting and you want to be certain that I don't do it again."

Undershooting is one type of intensity mismatch; we've also observed people who are prone to overshooting the speaker's emotional intensity. This raises the stakes needlessly:

He: *"I wish you'd drive more slowly."*
She: *"You think I'm a reckless maniac!"*
He: *"I didn't say that! But if the shoe fits…"*

In this scenario, the person being criticized obviously experienced the impact of the message in a very intense manner. But where was the act of listening to intent? What was being criticized was a behavior. But the listener applied an insulting label to himself, and drew out a far more negative communication than the speaker initially appeared to have in mind. The attempt to paraphrase went belly up. A response that truly reflected intent might have been, "I'm driving too fast for you and it's making you nervous."

We've also noticed that people who are just beginning to use the paraphrasing skill tend to have an upward inflection in their voice when they do it. When they say, "My speed is making you nervous," it comes out sounding like a question: *My speed is making you nervous?* Their tentative, questioning tone minimizes the power of paraphrasing. What's more, it can signal astonishment that the speaker could take such an outrageous position.

Finally, some people are over-ambitious with their paraphrasing. They jump ahead and anticipate the speaker, saying too much before the speaker has had time to get a complete message out ("Ooooh, ooh, stop, I already know what you mean."). They may also be tempted to offer solutions prematurely ("Ahh, got it. Say no more. I'll never do it again.

Case closed!"). Both of these approaches probably owe their genesis to the listener's desire to "just get this over with." And that is exactly how they come off. Better to take paraphrasing one step at a time, letting the speaker take the lead. Even if you are correct in knowing where the speaker is headed, that person will feel better understood if he gets to say what he needs to in his own words.

It's relatively easy to avoid the common pitfalls of paraphrasing simply by being aware of them. To paraphrase effectively:

- Listen carefully (a posture of curiosity will help).
- Discern what the speaker intends to convey and reflect it back.
- Avoid reiterating the same introductory phrase ("What I hear you saying is…").
- Avoid parroting the message word for word.
- Match emotional intensity.
- Make statements; don't use a questioning tone.
- Don't say too much.
- Don't rush to offer solutions.

With practice, you can become very adept at discovering and reflecting intent. Be aware, though, that often this skill will have to go hand in hand with another: asking for details.

Step 2: Ask for Details

Often, someone presenting a criticism will do so in an extremely general way: "I'm tired of you ridiculing me."

Because the criticism is so vague, the recipient truly doesn't know what the speaker is referring to. Nevertheless, instead of asking for clarification, defensive mode kicks in and the listener lobs back a reflexive retort. "I don't ridicule you."

What might follow is a volley: "Yes, you do." "No, I don't."

This might lead to an escalation and counter-accusation: "Yes, you do. You do it all the time." "No, I don't. You just take everything so personally. Why can't you lighten up?"

If, however, the listener remembered that the paradox of responding to criticism means asking for more information, then the dialogue might have gone something like this:

He: *"I'm tired of you ridiculing me."*
She: *"So it feels like I've been picking on you."* [paraphrasing]
He: *"Yes, that's right."*
She: *"Can you help me by letting me know what I've been doing to give you that impression?"* [asking for details]

What often follows is explicit clarifying information. The speaker may or may not agree with the details as stated by the critic; nevertheless, a lot more is known than was known before. A starting point for potential agreement is achieved.

Why don't we do this more often? Because, once again, we instinctively want to shut the speaker down when we are criticized. Though details help understanding, paradoxically, we feel we do not want them. Why should we? After all, details might interfere with our certainty that we are in the right.

The absence of details, though, is a serious flaw when it comes to arriving at a resolution. It's virtually impossible to agree to blanket criticisms or to negative labels. It's a rare individual (perhaps a masochistic or sarcastic one at that) who's simply going to roll over and say, "Hey, you're right. I'm an insensitive idiot!"

Details, on the other hand, are often extremely enlightening. Here's a continuation of the previous example:

"Last night at the dinner party, I was talking about how strongly I felt about protecting the environment. You said if I felt so sensitive to the environment I should get out and mow the lawn."

True? Not true? At least you *can* proceed from here because you've got something concrete to work with.

So, the second step in the Responding to Criticism model simply involves asking for details when a critic is speaking in general terms. Did we say simply? Let's amend that. As with assuming a posture of curiosity, you'll have to function counter-intuitively at first. When you ask for details, don't wince up and hold your breath. Open your body and open your mind to receive the information you've requested. It's all part of the discovery process.

One additional caveat: Be aware of your word choices and your tone of voice when asking for details. Is the relationship message *I really want to understand*, or *Prove it?* Reponses like "Oh yeah, name me one time—just one—when I ridiculed you" are not invitations to provide detail. They are exactly the opposite. They convey the relationship message: *You don't know what you're talking about. You're either wrong or stupid.*

Step 3: Guess

Sometimes speakers can respond to a request for details immediately. In other instances, they may be unable or unwilling to do so. Possibly they don't remember specifics because they've let their emotions build to a point where negative feelings are the sole focus. Possibly they feel embarrassed to enumerate specifics, thinking they may come off as petty. Possibly they are genuinely startled that you actually want to know more.

Whatever the reason, if a critic won't offer specifics, we urge listeners to once again take a counter-intuitive tack and guess. Help the critic to criticize more effectively.

> *"Did you feel neglected because I gave your birthday gift belatedly?"*

> *"Are you feeling jealous because I paid Phyllis so many compliments when she lost weight?"*

> *"Do you feel I play favorites because I let Jessica work from home twice a week?"*

This is a step that most people resist when they first hear it. *Isn't that giving the critic enough rope to hang me with? What if I suggest something they haven't even thought of yet?*

Paradoxically, this step tends to generate specific information that's needed in order to proceed, without escalating the situation. Why? Because at the very significant relationship level, the message that guessing conveys is: *I'm so committed to making this work that I'm willing to make myself more vulnerable.*

Step 4: Agree with Facts

Step 4 begins the next stage of our model: Seek Out Agreement. In most areas of life, it's safe to assume the people with whom we interact have some sort of agenda, just as we have our own. Sometimes individual goals and desires dovetail, but often—even in the most loving families, close-knit friendships, or synergistic organizations—people work at cross-purposes.

All of this is healthy. Imagine a family, a company, or a committee in which everyone agreed all the time. The result would be complacency, and ultimately, stagnation. No new information would ever be introduced into the system, no learning would take place, and nothing would evolve. If you're currently embroiled in a conflict you might think, hey, a little complacency and stagnation sounds a lot better than what I'm dealing with. But, in actuality, you'd shortly be bored out of your mind. Of course, the other extreme—perennial conflict without resolution—is equally undesirable. In this scenario, too, no learning or growth is achieved.

Agreement is the only way through and out of conflict. That desirable result begins when the conflicting parties agree on *something*. That's because even a tiny bit of agreement acts like a magnet: more and more concurrence will stick to it.

Step 4 of the Responding to Criticism model addresses this basic starting point: agree with facts. Facts are often the easiest thing to agree on.

When practicing this step, be explicit in your agreement. Use a neutral tone and objective language. Make it clear that, at this point, facts are all you're agreeing with:

Fact: *"Your birthday gift was late."*

Fact: *"I did pay Phyllis a lot of compliments."*

Fact: *"Jessica is the only person allowed to work from home during the week."*

There, that wasn't so hard, was it? It's the *interpretation* of facts, rather than facts themselves, that causes the most disagreement, which brings us to the next step in the process.

Step 5: Agree with the Critic's Perception

People perceive objects differently. The glass is half full; the glass is half empty. That Rorschach blot looks like a butterfly; it looks like two people kissing. People also perceive the behaviors of others differently. You laughed at my joke; you laughed at me. You didn't see me come in; you snubbed me.

Step 5 of the Responding to Criticism model urges the listener to agree with the critic's perception. *Acknowledge that the critic has a right to see things as he or she does.* Once we understand how critics interpreted the facts, we may come to feel that the way they behaved made sense *based on what they believed to be true about the situation*:

> *"I can see how my getting your present a week late would upset you, since I've never done that before and since I didn't mention that I even remembered your birthday."*

> *"I can see why my spending so much time telling Phyllis how great she looked made you think I was flirting with her."*

> *"I can see why my letting Jessica work from home makes it seem like I favor her over other employees."*

At this juncture there are two choices for attempting to reach resolution. One is to accept the critic's perception and agree to change your behavior. In such cases a simple apology goes a long way. "I'm glad you told me. I will commit to this change. In a couple of weeks, please give me some feedback and let me know how I'm doing."

The second choice is to clarify your own behavior so that the critic understands. This is a perfectly viable option. You may have had very valid reasons for acting as you did.

> *"The birthday present I got you was back-ordered and I didn't want to spoil the surprise."*

> *"Phyllis always puts herself down and I thought I could be a good friend by building her confidence."*

> *"I agreed to Jessica's telecommuting because she's a single mother and we agreed to this contingency plan when she started working here."*

No Buts About It

If the option of clarifying your behavior is the one you want to exercise, we do offer one caveat: Stay away from the word "but," as in: "I can understand how you feel, but…"

"But" is a loaded word because it signals that everything that came before it should be disregarded. If you've ever been the recipient of a message like "I'd like to keep going out with you, but…," or "I wish we could keep you on here at Omnibank, but…," you know exactly what we mean.

As an alternative you may want to consider phrases such as: "I can understand how you'd come to that conclusion. Here's how I saw it." Or: "I see how you came to your point of view and here's what was going on for me." Remember, this is a model rather than a formula. Improvise as needed and make the model work for you.

The Duration Effect

Another thing to bear in mind: Research tells us that people remember what they spend the most time talking about. Take advantage of this "duration effect." As you draw to the close of a conversation in which you've been responding to criticism, linger on points of agreement.

Even if you saw the situation differently than your critic and have said so, end by summing up the points on which you've concurred—the facts, and your critic's right to have perceived them as he did.

Speed Kills

Many of us have a tendency to speed through events we consider unpleasant, because that's how our defenses work. But when responding to criticism, don't be in a rush to conclude the conversation. In fact, be careful to pace all of your responses at a consistent and reasonably slow rate.

The overriding tasks in responding to criticism are to get more information and to seek out agreement. You can't do either when you're in a rush. When it comes to courting criticism and resolving conflict, the tortoise trumps the hare.

Putting It Together

In order to see how the Responding to Criticism model works as a whole, here's a before and after scenario. This is a situation we ran across when we were hired to consult at a busy title insurance company. The precipitating issue: one employee is allowed to work shorter hours than the rest. In the "before" scenario, the office staff was resentful and had stopped functioning well as a team. A typical conversation between a critical employee and the owner, Steve, would have gone something like this:

> **Fran:** *"Steve, I've got to tell you that something's really bothering me. And it's not just me. Everybody feels this way."*
> **Steve:** (sighing) *"All right, what now?"*
> **Fran:** *"You're always giving special perks to Amy and we don't think it's fair."*

Steve: *"Now, wait a minute. Amy has been here a long time. And anyway, it's none of your business. I wish you'd spend more time doing your job than worrying about other people."*

Fran: *"It is my business. It doesn't seem fair that we're all working here and supposedly part of a team. But one person on the team is your golden girl."*

Steve: *"Part of being a team is not running around behind people's backs and stabbing them at the first opportunity. If you did half the work Amy did, maybe you'd have more privileges here."*

In the "after" scenario, Steve gets more information by listening actively and asking for details—as well as guessing when they're not forthcoming. He then seeks agreement and explains his position while lingering on points of agreement.

Fran: *"Steve, I've got to tell you that something's really bothering me. And it's not just me. Everybody feels this way."*

Steve: *"What is it, Fran?"*

Fran: *"You're always giving special perks to Amy and we don't think it's fair."*

Steve: *"So, it seems like I'm playing favorites and that's upsetting you."*

Fran: *"Yes, it seems like she's the golden girl around here."*

Steve: *"Fran, can you help me out and let me know exactly where you feel that Amy is getting more privileges than you and the rest of the staff?"*

Fran: *"She comes and goes as she pleases. Two days a week she goes waltzing out while we're all up to our eyeballs here. She gets everything that she wants. In your eyes, Amy can do no wrong."*

Steve: *"I know one benefit Amy gets is going home at three o'clock twice a week."*

Fran: *"Yes. And she never has to work evenings."*

Steve: *"You're absolutely right. Amy does leave at three o'clock twice a week and never works evenings. I can see how that might seem unfair. What you may not know is that I hired Amy a number of years ago because she had extensive experience. She indicated that because she was a single mom, the most important thing to her was shorter, more flexible hours. That was our agreement."*

Fran: *"You're right. I wasn't aware of all that."*

Steve: *"I'm glad you brought it up. And if there's anything else I'm doing that seems unfair, please let me know. Because it's certainly not my intention."*

Will things always unfold this smoothly? Obviously, some personalities and situations offer up greater challenges than others. But the more this model is practiced, the more effective it will prove to be. Over time, defensive instincts yield to new habits. As a result, those who use the model tend to view critics and conflicts as less daunting. That self-assurance helps them use the models in ever more skillful ways. So a positive cycle is set in motion. The example in Leader Insight 4-3 demonstrates the powerful effects of reacting to conflict situations with intentional rather than automatic responses.

Leader Insight 4-3

The Power of Initial Silence in High Stakes Situations

After working to prepare over a thousand witnesses in legal settings for trial or deposition, at least one thing is very clear, says Dr. David Illig, President of Portland, Oregon's Litigation Psychology. "No matter how honest and sincere you are, or how smart and educated, the first thing that comes to your mind and out of your mouth is rarely the best thing that could be said to communicate your point of view."

Furthermore, says Illig, in a stressful, conflict-ridden situation, the likelihood is extremely low that we even heard the question or statement accurately the first time. "We respond to what we thought we heard, which is, about 50 percent of the time, not what was actually asked. This is a function of our brain mechanism and not indicative of a lack of intelligence or education. In fact, the quicker brain can more easily be fooled into poor listening—precisely because it's so fast.

"However, we *think* we heard the question or statement accurately," Illig explains. "We also think that our answer best portrays the truth. Good attorneys understand this, but they certainly won't tell you about it when they interrogate you. If you read back your transcript or watch a recording of yourself being interrogated, it's easier for you to notice."

Not everyone will be interrogated by a professional attorney in deposition or trial, but everyone deals with very stressful situations where there is some element of conflict and some element of adversarial competition and the stakes are high. What is the solution? To be faster, smarter, more knowledgeable than the person interrogating you?

"No," says Illig. "My experience, in working with hundreds of intellectually gifted physicians, is that being faster, smarter, or more knowledgeable doesn't work. The only thing that consistently works is to slow the whole process down. *Silence* is the safest and best way to move the brain and nervous system from automatic reactions to intentional responses that communicate what you mean to say.

"Silence is difficult, rare, and powerful. Humans are addicted to speed and talk, especially under stress. It's just the nature of our brain."

Illig continues: "Try this pattern. In stressful conflict situations, do not respond with any words until after a count of three. It will feel like a count of ten. Just act as if you are a poor listener (everybody is partially, because we all rush). Do this even when you think it's unnecessary. Silently inspect what you initially thought was said and determine what was really said. Fifty percent of the time you'll reevaluate.

"Next," Illig says, "do a two-step on your response. Look at what your brain initially threw out as an answer. Consider whether it actually does the best job of communicating the truth you want to get across. At least half the time you can do better. Create a second or third option and pick the best option for accomplishing what you want to communicate. Your mind is pretty busy during this review. Now you can open your mouth and say it."

Illig allows that this technique is difficult and isn't practical in all communication. "However, in high-stakes situations, where each word really matters, this is an invaluable pattern to learn. It takes a great deal of practice. It never feels entirely comfortable, but you can *appear* comfortable while you ponder. Your two-step response doesn't look as strange to others as it feels to you. Don't be self-conscious. After all, why shouldn't you be careful and meticulous in high-stakes conflict situations?"

Choose some content and practice this technique over and over, Illig advises. "This will give you a huge advantage over people who don't have this skill. Practice it in the grocery store, or the gas station, or the restaurant, on any trivial content just to learn the pattern. The behavior is much more difficult than the concept. Most people are terrified of silence. *Silence is your friend.* Quick responses are automatic; slowed responses will be intentional. When you finally say what you have decided to say using this pattern, you will notice that it feels different speaking out of intent rather than speaking straight from the automatic nervous system.

"Where the stakes are *not* high," Illig concludes, "it's fine to give quick automatic responses, catching any slips later with little damage done. Use the two-step method in dangerous, risky, scary, important, or potentially costly situations."

As with all of our models, this one doesn't stand alone. Just as each of us is sometimes criticized, each of us also has some legitimate complaints or concerns about the behavior of others. Our next chapter shows how influential communicators can raise delicate issues while preserving—and strengthening—their relationships.

Chapter Five

Who Woke the Dogs Up?
Raising Delicate Issues

It's harder to give than to receive—criticism, that is. As challenging as it is to respond calmly and productively to criticism, many of us consider it more challenging still to raise delicate matters that we sense might upset the status quo of our relationships.

Oddly, many of us embrace a double standard when it comes to this proactive means of addressing and resolving conflict. Most people we've ever questioned on the subject say *they would want to know* if they had done something to offend someone with whom they had a relationship. Yet even people who place a high value on this desire admit they are reluctant to perform the same service for others. If an associate, friend, or family member has behaved in a way that has upset us, we're often inclined to let sleeping dogs lie rather than bring the matter up and put the relationship at risk. The rationalizations we make for avoiding sensitive subjects are voluminous. *We don't want to be impolite. We don't have the time to get into it. We don't want to look like the bad guy. We don't want to do damage to the relationship. We don't want to hurt anyone's feelings. We hope the problem will just go away.* Most of all, we're just plain scared.

The trouble with letting sleeping dogs lie, though, is that we have to keep stepping over them. If we don't tiptoe gingerly, we're in danger of rousing those puppies and then…well, who knows? As a result of our sidestepping, a silence often develops around small "unspeakable" issues. That silence can spread, and even spiral out of control. Now the relatively minor issue we've been avoiding has, seemingly of its own accord, expanded to encompass every nursed grudge and stored grievance that ever existed in the history of the relationship.

Sensitive subjects can, and do, crop up in all ongoing relationships. All of us can recall points in our lives when our personal or professional bonds suffered as a result of a small misunderstanding that escalated with the passage of time. There was that time when your best friend (or former best friend) flirted with your date, the time your coworker (whom you now shun) took credit for something you'd accomplished, the time when your sister-in-law (to whom you now barely speak) served shrimp at a holiday dinner—even though you're allergic to shellfish. Such events, annoying and upsetting though they may be, don't by themselves mandate the end of a long-term relationship that's been positive overall. But all too often that's what happens when we're afraid to address one transgression.

A Matter of Trust

What is it that we most fear about raising sensitive subjects? The answer seems to revolve around trust, and what we *imagine* begets trust between people. Most of us equate trust in relationships with lack of discord. People trust us because they get along with us and because we're nice to them, right?

Wrong.

They may no longer trust us if we bring a problem to their attention, right?

Wrong again.

We don't mean to suggest that getting along and being nice are undesirable goals. We all enjoy having an air of overall pleasantness and ease in relationships. But heartfelt trust—the firm belief that someone will act honorably, responsibly, and fairly—can only develop as a result of a deeper sort of dialogue.

The more we're able to tell people what's on our minds, and to do so in a nonthreatening manner, the more they'll be inclined to respond openly. This dynamic lays a bedrock foundation that will hold firm even on those days when things may not be so very pleasant on the surface, and when people don't necessarily see eye to eye.

Often when the moment comes to air a delicate issue, we wonder: Does this person trust me enough to take this in? If we fear that answer is *no*, that our bond isn't strong enough, we'll lose our nerve and back away. But here is the paradox: Courageous communication requires forging ahead anyhow, secure in the knowledge that *trust is not a prerequisite for communication; trust is a byproduct of communication.*

Remember too: It only takes one person to change a system. As one part moves, the others move to accommodate the change.

A Model for Raising Delicate Issues

In order to thrive on conflict, we must be able to raise sensitive issues in such a way that people will readily engage in a conversation and work with us toward a solution. Since we already know how likely most people are to assume a defensive position—physically, mentally, and emotionally—when faced with criticism, it stands to reason that our persuasive powers will be greater if we bring up whatever the matter is in a way that minimizes the listener's resistance.

Our model for raising delicate issues allows you to give critical feedback without getting people overly defensive or upset. It consists of four steps, which we'll lay out here and then elaborate on. [see Figure 5-A on page 88]

A Model for
Raising Delicate Issues—Summary

 Opener—Psychological agreement to have the conversation

I-Feeling Language—When people feel pushed, it creates a counter-resistance

Edit Accusative Language—Look for loaded language and red-flag terms

 Pinpoint Details—Tell people exactly what they said and when they said it, or exactly what they did and when they did it

 Acknowledge Your Part—Search for and communicate how you've contributed to the problem

 Agree on a Solution—Develop a solution that you both create and both implement

Figure 5-A

Step 1

Opener: Obtain psychological agreement to have the conversation.

> **EXAMPLE:** *"Can I talk to you about something I've been concerned about?"*
>
> ☞ **Note:** Talk in private, sitting down if possible.

I-Feeling language: Avoid "you" language, which pushes people to retaliate.

> **EXAMPLE:** *"I'm feeling underutilized."*
> **Not:** *"You never give me any good assignments."*
>
> **EXAMPLE:** *"I'm embarrassed."*
> **Not:** *"You always put me down."*
>
> ☞ **Note:** It's not a feeling if you can put the word *that* after the word *feel* (*"I feel that you're excluding me"*), or if you can substitute the word think for the word feel (*"I think you're being unfair"*).

Edit Accusative Language: Be on the lookout for loaded language and red-flag terms.

> **EXAMPLE:** *"I'm upset because I feel misunderstood."*
> **Not:** *"You never listen to me. You always overrule me."*

Step 2

Pinpoint Details: Tell people exactly what they said and when they said it, or exactly what they did and when they did it.

> **EXAMPLE:** *"Yesterday when you phoned the clients about the delay in getting edits to the marketing plan, you raised your voice and told the office manager she was incompetent."*

Not: *"The way you talk on the phone is curt and overbearing."*

EXAMPLE: *"Last week you told me and another coworker how stupid it was for Julie to send out the wrong report."*
Not: *"You bad-mouth people and put them down."*

EXAMPLE: *"When I asked you whether you had finished your part of the strategic plan, you said, 'I haven't gotten to it yet—so leave me alone.'"*
Not: *"You snapped at me and took my head off."*

EXAMPLE: *"When I asked you if you were upset with me, you said everything was fine. Then our supervisor called me in to tell me that you thought I wasn't doing my full share."*
Not: *"You're passive-aggressive. You're friendly to my face but then drop bombs with our supervisor. I can't trust you."*

Compared to generalized complaints, pinpointing specifics is:
- less intimidating
- more educational

Step 3
Acknowledge Your Part: Determine and communicate how you've contributed to the problem.

> **EXAMPLE:** *"I know I own part of this problem too, because at the meeting I stayed focused on my plan even when I could see the group was advocating a different course of action."*

Acknowledging your part of the problem is powerful because:
- It releases the other person from feeling blamed.
- It allows you to see the conflict from the other person's perspective.
- It encourages the other person to accept his part in the problem, since that's what you've done.

Step 4

Agree on a Solution: Avoid a vague or one-sided solution where one person does all the work.

- Begin with your part in the solution.
  EXAMPLE: *"Here's what I can do to make this work..."*
- Ask if there is anything else the other person would like you to do.
- Describe what you would like the other person to do.
  EXAMPLE: *"What I ask of you..."*

Timing May Not Be All, But It's a Lot

The first step in this model advises you to "obtain psychological agreement to have the conversation." Naturally, it's logical to raise a delicate issue when the other person a) has time to talk with you and b) is not too stressed or distracted to focus on the conversation. That said, let's think about what kind of state *you* might be in when you make your opening gambit.

As we know, it takes courage to alter our longstanding habit of avoidance to air a sensitive subject. To one degree or another, raising an issue involves psyching ourselves up—especially if we don't do it very often. We remind ourselves of the good things that will come out of the process and of the harm that may result if we don't take this action. We rehearse what we're going to say in our heads. We try to mentally and emotionally prepare to further the conversation in light of what we imagine possible responses might be. Now we've built up our internal momentum. We're ready to face this challenge. Good and ready. We want to go ahead while we're in the mood, and before we lose our resolve. *But, wait...*we still need to take the other party's emotional temperature. Just because we're ready to talk doesn't mean other people are ready to hear us.

So, look before you leap. Is the other person:
- in the midst of dealing with an unrelated problem?
- overly burdened with work, duties, or tasks?

- overwhelmed by some personal crisis?
- feeling physically ill?
- feeling tired?
- pressed for time?
- getting ready to leave for a much-anticipated weekend or vacation break?

If the answer is yes to any of the above—not to mention if the person you plan to speak with has just had her car rear-ended, just had a bird relieve itself on his new suit, or recently gave up smoking or chocolate—this is *not* the time to raise a delicate matter. No matter how fully prepared you are, insensitivity to timing will set the stage for a frustrating encounter.

Even if you think you know the answer, be sure to inquire if the time is a good one for talking. Pay attention not only to the verbal response you receive but also to body language. Sometimes people will agree to talk even when they're in an exceptionally foul humor, just to get "one more thing out of the way." Remember the power of nonverbal communication to signal genuine intent. If their words say *yes* but their rigid body posture or tapping foot says *not really*, take your cue from the latter. Indicate you'd rather wait until another time, and set that time mutually so that your opportunity arrives in the near future.

I-Feelings and Self-Disclosure

Our model also advises using I-feeling language. The temptation when critiquing someone else's behavior is to speak in the second person. *You do this and you do that.* The listener perceives each and every "you" as a tiny poison arrow. As soon as the sting is felt, the listener starts to pull away or gear up for a counter-attack. Flight or fight, as usual.

Speaking in the first person is a far less threatening approach. Yet many of us are uncomfortable with this because we equate self-disclosure with vulnerability. How much we say about ourselves and to whom we say it does present a quandary.

There's no definitive research that tells us the optimal amount of self-disclosure. Relationships differ, and comfort levels of individuals vary. However, we do know that disclosing too much personal material too soon can have a negative impact. Sit down next to a stranger on an airplane and reveal your innermost fears, hopes, and fantasies, and you'll soon have your seatmate feigning sleep or retreating behind an iPod. Tell a first date what you want to name your three children and there may not be a second date.

Still, when using this model, *you* have made the decision to raise a sensitive subject with someone you interact with on a regular basis. Your goal is to get that person to give you a fair hearing. Some degree of self-disclosure is the means to that end. The feelings that you should reveal are the ones that are immediately relevant. While it's not necessary, or desirable, to enumerate every feeling you've had over the course of your entire relationship, it is important that you describe how you feel about the situation. If you don't, the process of building trust is stymied from the start.

Self-disclosure, of course, requires self-awareness. Because we're complicated creatures, it's sometimes difficult to know exactly what our primary emotion is, let alone put it into words. We've found that one of the most common mistakes made in raising sensitive subjects is that instead of *describing* feelings, people *ascribe* them. They say things like: "You make me feel anxious/depressed/unwelcome." This is not true self-disclosure; it's merely a way of designating blame.

Equally as counter-productive are statements that begin with the words *I feel that*. If you can put the word *that* after the word *feel*, or if you can substitute the word *think* for *feel*, what comes next is usually a thought and not a feeling. The worst example of this we've ever seen was when a gentleman who struggled long and hard to come up with a self-disclosing statement finally blurted out in frustration, "I feel that…you're an idiot!"

A complete list of possible feelings would go on for a very, very long time. The following group of primary feelings is meant only to provide you with an idea of what we are referring to when we speak about using I-feelings. [see Figure 5-B on page 95]

Forbidden Phrases

The initial step of our model concludes by advising that we edit out blatantly accusatory language. Just as it's possible for a list of feelings to go on indefinitely, it's possible to endlessly dream up words and phrases that provoke people. There are some so inflammatory, however, that we thought we'd mention them.

When airing sensitive subjects, steer clear of any language implying that a person's objectionable behavior is something that *always* occurs. Likewise, don't tell people that they *never* behave well. These kinds of sweeping, all-or-nothing statements indicate that the situation is hopeless. With such a global premise in place, a constructive dialogue can't possibly follow.

Similarly, remember that you're broaching a *subject* rather than attacking someone's *character*. Stay away from blanket descriptions of negative behavior. People don't want to hear that they:

- put other people down
- don't plan ahead
- treat everyone like children
- have an attitude problem
- like to interrupt
- bite people's heads off
- take advantage
- avoid problems
- snub people

Primary Feelings

afraid
alarmed
alone
anxious
apathetic
appreciated
awkward
bewildered
calm
closed
comfortable
committed
compassionate
competent
concerned
confident
confused
curious
cut off from others
defeated
dejected
dependent
depressed
disappointed
eager
embarrassed
enthusiastic
excited
exhilarated

fearful
glad
grateful
guilty
happy
hopeful
hopeless
impatient
inadequate
incompetent
indecisive
inferior
inhibited
insecure
involved
isolated
jealous
joyful
lonely
loved
loving
melancholy
misunderstood
needy
optimistic
overwhelmed
pessimistic
phony
playful

pleased
possessive
preoccupied
prejudiced
pressured
protective
proud
rejected
remorseful
restrained
sad
secure
shallow
shy
stubborn
stupid
supported
supportive
sympathetic
terrified
threatened
tolerant
torn
unsure
unresponsive
useless
weepy
wishy-washy
well

Figure 5-B

In addition, refrain from labeling people with such terms as:

- rigid
- bossy
- nit-picky
- moody
- inflexible
- selfish
- stand-offish
- arrogant
- impatient
- intimidating
- obnoxious
- critical
- close-minded
- judgmental
- rude
- unsupportive
- controlling
- unfriendly

Obviously, name-calling of this or any sort is insulting. Moreover, to call people such things describes an expectation that *you* hold for *their* behavior. We've already discussed how such expectations can be self-fulfilling. Tell people they're always rude, and you can practically guarantee they'll be rude to you henceforth. Now your chances of successfully raising a delicate subject have vanished into thin air.

Keep in mind too that if you call people "nitpicky and rigid," they honestly won't know what you're referring to because they don't think of themselves in those kinds of terms. Seeing themselves instead as detail-oriented, professional, and precise, they are confused—and defensive—when faced with your label.

Details are the Antidote to Accusations

The second step in our model, talking about specifics, is the antidote to making other people feel blamed and accused on a character level. Think of pinpointing as a teaching tool. When you describe details relating to a situation, you educate people about their *behavior* and the impact it has on you. The more concrete your description, the better.

> **Unproductive:** *"You're a spendthrift."*
> **Slightly Better:** *"You spent too much money last month."*
> **MUCH BETTER:** *"Last month, you overdrew the checking account by two hundred and twenty dollars."*

The more you pinpoint facts, the less likely you are to provoke an automatic defensive reaction.

It Takes Two

The third step in our model, acknowledging your part, is instructive. Before you bring up the sensitive subject you have in mind, take some time to reflect on what *your* role in the matter was and how it may have contributed to the problem at hand. We know that at first blush it may seem to you that you are completely innocent.

Think harder.

Acknowledging your part is essentially an exercise in empathy. To succeed you will have to project yourself, metaphorically at least, into other people's mindsets. What might they have seen in *your* actions that prompted them to act as they did? If someone interrupted you, ask yourself if you might have a tendency to talk on for too long. If someone didn't include you in an event, ask yourself if you've always included that person.

We're not suggesting that you publicly flagellate yourself, or take responsibility for wrongs you plainly didn't commit. All you really need to do is let other people see that you don't view yourself as perfect, while viewing them as tragically flawed. A way to get to the part you play is to ask yourself: If they were talking to their friend about you and the situation, how might they characterize events?

Approaching a sensitive discussion in a more empathic frame of mind helps the other person feel less "muscled" and more receptive. It will also serve to calm you down before you begin to air a sensitive issue. Anxiety can be contagious. The less agitated you are, the less the likelihood of spreading negative emotions.

Avoiding Problems in Solutions

So, what's the purpose of raising a delicate matter anyway? If you do it successfully, you may clear up a misunderstanding or even receive an apology. But in most cases the ultimate purpose of raising a sensitive matter is to ensure that, whatever the problem was, it will be resolved. Before the discussion is over, the makings of a solution should evolve. *Make sure the other person understands that you value this relationship and want it to continue as harmoniously as possible.* But beware: So-called solutions can generate more problems if planning for them isn't thoughtfully and diplomatically handled.

One common mistake people make is coming up with a so-called plan that is vague and open-ended. Steps that are required to put a constructive solution in place should be clearly outlined, and a time frame delineated.

> **Unproductive:** *"So, let's figure out a way to do something about it."*
> **Slightly Better:** *"Let's consider having household budget meetings once in a while."*
> **MUCH BETTER:** *"Suppose we agree to sit down together the first of each month and talk about our anticipated income and expenses."*

If clarity is lacking, other matters will take priority, or basic inertia will kick in. In either case, things will go back to the way they were before. Don't let this opportune moment to craft a workable plan slip through your fingers.

A second flawed, though common, scenario is when the person raising the issue in the first place single-handedly concocts a solution, the work of which must be done entirely by the other person.

> **Unproductive:** *"So here's my plan. You submit a spending plan at the beginning of each month that shows how our budget will last for the month."*
>
> **Slightly Better:** *"What do you think about developing a spending plan together that we can look at the first of each month?"*
>
> **MUCH BETTER:** *"One idea I have is to work together and create a monthly spending plan. What do you think of that idea? What else can you and I agree to do?"*

For a solution to be effective in this situation, it must be one that both parties create and both parties implement. *Each person needs a voice in developing the solution and a job to do when the conversation is over.*

Tell the other party what you can contribute to a solution, then ask and suggest what he might do. Always conclude by asking if there is anything else he would like you to do. This last query often yields some constructive suggestions concerning the way you communicate. People who have used this model have reported to us they have received valuable suggestions, such as how it would be helpful to discuss an incident closer to the time it occurred, or to initiate more face-to-face contact and rely less on email. Giving the other person permission to have the last word reaffirms that you value him, and so elicits a level of feedback you may never have otherwise received.

The Fifty-One Percent Rule

Speaking of last words, one helpful overall technique in raising sensitive subjects is to let the other person speak more than you do. It doesn't have to be a lot more, but let her do the talking 51 percent of the time.

We don't expect anyone to parse words or to carry on a conversation with the aid of a stop watch. What we do suggest is that you go in with the *intent* of allotting the other person a majority of the time. Watch for the natural break points in your own discourse. When you come to the end of a thought, *take a breath* before launching into your next one. Use this brief pause to notice the other person's expression and body language. Does it appear that something is on the tip of her tongue? Then bite your own tongue for another moment and give her the opportunity to say it.

Letting the other person speak more than you makes her feel more empowered and lessens fears that she is being chastised. It also gives you time to collect your thoughts and to incorporate new information as you go along. Again, our recommendation is to let the other party do most of the talking. Paradoxically, you will be more persuasive.

The Sensitive Subject Model in Action

We already know that any enduring relationship is prone to sensitive subjects. Both businesses and families have their "unspeakables"—leading to unresolved problems and bruised feelings. When we were considering an example of a before-and-after case to illustrate how to communicate about delicate issues, though, we decided to offer the following scenarios that took place in a family-owned business.

Throughout our careers, we have worked extensively with family businesses. They can be uniquely challenging in that their communication systems encompass both personal and professional issues, which can often overlap. Consider this "before" scenario, in which Janet raised a sensitive subject with her business partner and husband, John. The matter involved John's brother, Tim, the production manager of a wood products manufacturing plant.

> **Janet:** *"You know, I need to get this off my chest, so let me get right to the point. You just can't let your brother keep dominating you the way he has been. I mean, you're the president of this company. Tim's*

only the production manager, but he can do anything he wants. He's just running the show."

John: *"Here we go again. We've been married for twenty-six years and you're still jealous of the relationship I have with my brother. It's okay, honey, you can let it go now."*

Janet: *"You think I'm jealous of the relationship you have with your brother? What relationship? He tells you what to do and you do it!"*

John: *"That doesn't even warrant a response."*

Janet: *"Your Neanderthal brother is ruining the morale of everyone on staff. He goes into the plant, he intimidates people, puts them down and harasses them. And you act as though you are deaf, dumb, and blind."*

John: *"Hey, Timmy is a little rough around the edges. He's not going to win any congeniality awards. I know that. But he's basically doing a decent job. He doesn't let the crew get off early. He makes sure they return from their breaks on time. He's running a tight ship. I know sometimes the morale..."*

Janet: *"Morale is in the toilet! But what do you care? I give up. I'm tired of being the only compassionate person around here."*

Much went awry in this misguided attempt to broach a sensitive subject. If Janet had good intentions, they were certainly never heard. Not only was she unsuccessful in this dialogue, she ensured that her husband would be unsuccessful as well. She jumped head first into the conversation, and provoked John by calling him and his brother names and by making over-generalized accusations. When we push on people they push back—often harder—as John did. Finally, Janet attributed no responsibility to herself in this situation and proposed no solutions.

Now consider how this matter could have been raised once Janet practiced our model for raising delicate issues.

Opener: *"John, is this a good time to talk to you about something that's been on my mind?"*

Describe feelings/edit accusations: *"I'm very worried about Tim's relationship with the production crew."*

Pinpoint details: *"Yesterday, when Tim was on the production floor, he thought two of the guys were taking too long getting back from their break. He picked up a wrench and threw it against the wall, not far from where they were standing. Later, I overheard the two of them talking about quitting, or even filing charges. And John, these are two of our best guys."*

Acknowledge your part: *"I know that I own part of this problem because things like this have happened before and I've been afraid to tell Tim myself. I've even had trouble mentioning them to you. I've also allowed Tim's crew to complain to me about this sort of behavior without encouraging them to speak to him directly."*

Agree on a solution: *"I'm going to meet with Tim and then ask his people to communicate directly with him as well. Can you think of anything else I should be doing? And I'd really appreciate it if you would talk to Tim about the impact of aggressive behavior in the workplace on safety and morale, not to mention production. Perhaps we can all meet then and discuss other options and actions. Let's get back together on this after we've both had a chance to speak with Tim."*

In this "after" scenario, Janet was careful to obtain John's agreement to have the conversation. She steered clear of insults and accusations, and instead offered a concrete example of her concerns. Remembering that every issue has two sides, she described how she had contributed to the problem by avoiding confrontation with Tim at an earlier time. She also remembered that every solution, like every problem, requires participation by both involved parties. So she asked for John's input and they created a collaborative agreement in which each person knew what to do in order to correct the situation.

Confronting delicate problems with business associates *or* family members is never an easy matter. But avoidance is worse. Sidestepping issues can lead to undeclared wars that can ravage enterprises and personal relationships. Paradoxically, persuasive communicators must "wake the dogs up" and choose directness—albeit directness that is carefully considered and thoughtfully orchestrated. These courageous efforts will be rewarded with creative solutions, increased closeness, and family systems and work teams that function at the highest possible levels.

Chapter Six

Gratitude:

Unleashing the Power of Encouragement

So far, we've explored a number of skills that have an impact on how you listen to people, how you understand and respond to their points of view, and how you can work with them to avoid misunderstandings. The fact that you've stuck with the program through this point, tolerating all of the awkward feelings that arise as you try out new and unfamiliar behaviors, leads us to make some educated guesses about you. First, we think you genuinely care about your relationships and put great stock in maintaining and improving them. Second, we think you sincerely value, appreciate, and admire other people.

Now we come to a model that will help you express how thankful you are to the many people who enhance your life, both at work and outside of it. This is our Gratitude and Recognition model.

Your Mother Was Right—and Then Some

We know we're not the first to mention how appropriate it is to say thank you. The virtues of this practice were doubtless extolled by your mother, who believed that expressions of gratitude would result in people realizing what a nice and well brought up person you were. We agree. But we also want to point out that communicating your recognition of others' contributions has even greater pay-offs than people recognizing your good manners. The following is a list of the greatest payoffs:

- **Concentration on praise, recognition, and reinforcement can change the chemistry of any organization or family system.** When people realize that their effort will be noticed and commented upon, their mood and attitude undergo a dramatic shift. Morale is lifted and the general atmosphere lightens. People function at higher levels with less inherent stress.

- **An environment rich in recognition and reinforcement makes dealing with conflict easier.** Practicing the art of praise will not solve every problem, but when a disagreement does arise, there is a reservoir of good feeling to draw upon that lessens negativity. The greater this reservoir, the speedier and more productive the resolution.

- **The reservoir of reinforcement makes it easier to raise delicate issues.** While a culture that integrates gratitude is not free of sore spots, sensitive subjects will be raised sooner—and hence dealt with more effectively—when a positive, gratitude-infused culture is in place.

- **Tell people you like what they're doing and they'll repeat it.** This simple principle is a cornerstone of behavioral psychology: Whatever gets positively reinforced gets repeated. The principle works equally well whether you're praising a coworker for fielding an important call in your absence or telling your teenage kids you appreciate it when they remember to gas up your car.

Our research and experience have shown that offering praise not only gets people to engage in the same behaviors again, but also to look for ways of improving upon them. As a Nigerian proverb has it: "Give thanks for a little and you will find a lot."

So what does this all mean? When we build gratitude and appreciation into our workplaces, homes, and schools, we begin to notice, and generate, more of what we want. Paradoxically, this is not what we typically do. Once again, our basic instincts get in the way of what we really want.

The "Uh-Oh" Factor

Our brains are wired to notice things that are out of alignment. Anything out of the ordinary can be interpreted as a potential threat or problem, and paying heed to such things is a reflexive mechanism. From a pure survival standpoint, this make sense. Primitive people, taking a walk through the brush, would have made a tasty meal for any carnivorous beast—had they not paid attention to sights, sounds, or smells that warned them of its presence. Even in our urban jungles, we are primed to be alert for screeching sirens, the smell of smoke, the menacing look of a stranger standing too close. The brain says "uh-oh," and we take protective measures accordingly.

This "uh-oh" mentality follows us everywhere. At the office, we're often so fixated on problems it's not uncommon to say we spent the day "putting out fires." At home, we seem to move from one hindrance to the next—the unpaid bill, the leaky faucet, the burned-out light bulb over the basement stairs. We're not knocking survival instincts, nor advocating that problems or nuisances be left untended. But we also know it's desirable to expand our realm of attention so that we also notice what *is* working.

When we flick a light switch and no light comes on, when we turn our ignition key and our car doesn't start, when we boot up our computer and—*uh oh!*—the screen remains dark, we have an unmet expectation. Typically, that unmet expectation causes us to voice our dismay. In short, our first response is to complain. On the other hand, when everything goes the way we anticipate that it should, we often don't notice it and usually don't mention it.

Most of us like to think we're grateful when things go well in our lives, but the fact is we're usually too busy thinking about what might go wrong. Most of us also like to think we express our thanks to the people who help keep our lives on an even keel—but how often do we actually take the time to do this?

Most people say they enjoy receiving recognition, yet recognition is rarely given. Can you recall the last time you were thanked for an effort you made? Okay, now can you think of the last time this happened in anything more than a cursory fashion?

Paradoxically, many people have some genuine concerns about being too free with their thanks. Some people have expressed a reticence to say thank you because they "don't want to look as though they're playing favorites." Others say they don't wish to inflate expectations: "Compliments can make employees think they're going to get a raise, and that's not always realistic." On occasion, we've even run across managers who equate praise with spoiling or coddling people. Their attitude is, "Of course employees ought to work hard and contribute. If you make a big deal out of it, they'll think that's the exception instead of the norm."

It's possible to anticipate negative consequences of even the most constructive actions. But in the case of gratitude, the potential upside is so enormous that it far outweighs any objections. The primary effect of gratitude is to offer encouragement—which is among the greatest incentives in existence.

Some Reprogramming Guidelines

Kicking the old habit of noticing only what's out of place—while taking all the things that work for granted—requires some reprogramming. It's not enough to remind ourselves to be grateful. Better to have some guidelines for developing a new habit of offering praise and reinforcement. Here are six guidelines that can be put into practice immediately by anyone who wishes to tap into the vast power of encouragement:

1. Look for opportunities for sincere praise.

Praiseworthy efforts are being made all around us every day. Noticing them is a matter of mindset. Some people find it helpful to make a daily practice of jotting down at least one thing that merits gratitude, and to check that item off when the appropriate person is thanked. This may be too formal a discipline for some, but it's an excellent way to jumpstart this habit change.

Opportunities for praise seem to present themselves more readily to those who make a conscious effort to remember that we are all interdependent on one another. As coworkers, family members, friends, and members of a community, we all rely upon one another to function in every aspect of our lives. Even most of the activities we perform "all by ourselves" would be virtually impossible unless others had contributed to the experience. If you're reading this book right now, it could be because some of the people who rely on you to do things are being kind enough to give you a respite from those duties so you can read in peace. If so, you might want to note and reinforce their good intentions.

2. Catch people doing right.

As all of us know, it's easy to get caught red-handed. All we need to do is think back to our days as children and most of us can readily recall instances of being told to *stand up straight* and *get rid of that chewing gum* and *stop talking*. Rarely did anyone tell us, "Hey, you've got awfully good posture for a little tyke, and you're pretty well behaved too." Sadly, most of us seem to have imprinted on this dynamic. Now, we too are prone to catch people doing things wrong.

Here's an opposite approach: We know of a large company where managers circulate through their departments several times a week saying, "Update me on what people have been doing to contribute to the success of your department." At the end of the week, each of those managers writes at least two or three notes of appreciation to those employees.

To generate a similar habit of positive reinforcement, make it your business to catch people doing things well, doing things enthusiastically, doing things thoughtfully. Before long you'll notice the people around you gaining confidence and energy—and doing even more things better.

3. Keep encouragement pure.

Perhaps you've heard of a popular management technique known as a "praise sandwich." With this method, managers are instructed to offer employees a compliment, follow it with a correction, and then finish up with another compliment. The result might be something like, "Ken, you did a great job on that special sales promotion last month. Your work was very effective there. But I haven't seen that same competence in the way you service your regular accounts. Again, exceptional job with that special campaign."

If Ken is like most people, we suspect he is undernourished by this praise sandwich. In fact, we wouldn't blame him if he felt a bit resentful of its mixed message. Ken's good work is not being so much recognized as held over his head. Is that really an incentive to repeat or expand his best efforts?

Unfortunately, the widespread use of the praise sandwich technique has created a culture of people waiting for the other shoe to drop. We emphatically suggest you forego this method in favor of pure encouragement: "Ken, you did an exceptional job with last month's special sales promotion. I believe the creativity you put into that campaign and the visibility you gave it contributed to raising our gross sales by 15 percent last quarter. Well done." (If Ken is having trouble servicing his regular accounts, that issue can be raised at another time.)

To be most effective, offerings of recognition must be served up in an unadulterated fashion. When we're praised for doing a good job in one area, that alone will often suffice to make us want to expand our efforts.

4. Focus on specific information.

Notice that Ken's second round of praise for the special sales promotion contained another feature in addition to its purity. It was more than a string of adjectives; instead, it included very specific details as to what was effective (Ken was creative and obtained visibility) and what the results were (a contribution to increased profits for the quarter).

Specificity in praise serves two very important functions. First, the praise feels more genuine and believable to its recipient. Second, people now know exactly which behaviors to repeat if more praise is desired.

5. Be a compliment messenger.

One of the most effective ways to create a positive culture is to fill one's environment with a pipeline of good news. Sadly, most of the things we find ourselves repeating about others are disagreeable. We dwell on who neglected to do what, who got into an argument with whom, who's in the doghouse. Whether fact or conjecture, whenever there's "dirt" we feel compelled to "dish it."

Humans gossip by nature. Evolutionary biologists theorize that gossip serves the same function in our society as grooming does among the lower primates: It's a method of remaining connected to a group. Based on this, eliminating gossip is not a realistic or desirable goal. But if we were to feed the gossip mill with positive tidings, the changes reflected back would be remarkable.

Instead of dishing dirt, repeat good stories you hear about anyone—and tell them to everyone who will listen. At first this will strike people as strange, about as strange as turning on the six o'clock news and hearing about good deeds and selfless acts versus criminal acts of violence. But after a while, this new standard can become the norm, to the benefit of all.

6. Praise in multiple directions.

We tend to think of praise moving primarily in a downward direction. Teachers praise students; managers praise people who report to them. While that's a vital activity, it's also important to praise upward. If your supervisor does something that enables you to do your job better, recognizing and reinforcing that supervisory activity will encourage similar behavior in the future. If your professor has taught in such a way as to spark your interest in a particular subject, say so. The feedback will go a long way toward keeping up that instructor's energy and enthusiasm—and you will have created a positive cycle.

Finally, be sure to offer horizontal recognition—department to department, section to section, shift to shift. This serves a very important function in that it strengthens lateral communication, which is by far the weakest link in most organizations.

People bask in praise and recognition like sea lions in the sun. They can happily soak it up all day. The power of such positive reinforcement is vast. Investing a small amount of time in looking for opportunities to praise, and then doing so, will never fail to generate a significant return. In Leader Insight 6-1, a college president uses his authority to give recognition with positive, long-range effects.

Leader Insight 6-1

The Heightened Impact of Recognition Given by Leaders

One day a young man approached University of Oregon president David Frohnmayer as he stood waiting to pick up his daughter from a tennis match. The man thanked him for "changing his life." Frohnmayer had no idea what he was referring to.

"It was about five years ago," the young man said. "I was a student at the U of O—struggling, young for my age, and insecure. One day I was walking across campus and you came out of that building with the big pillars on it. You just greeted and started talking to me. I felt I was important. 'The president of the university is talking to me!' That really made a difference. I felt I belonged at the university."

Frohnmayer, who had received similar feedback from time to time, began reflecting. "It made me realize that leaders have to be especially aware of ways in which they communicate to people, with or without words. Because of your title and authority—more than your personality—the impact you have is heightened. It is magnified. That must be in your consciousness. In the case of this young man, my talking with him was simple, literal recognition, rather than a special compliment. Imagine the power of a compliment!"

Frohnmayer is keenly aware that expressing thanks to people is one of the most reinforcing kinds of communication in which a leader can engage. "To this day I give out little gold stars to people when I send them a personal thank-you note. It may sound hokey, but people really appreciate that gesture. It reinforces what I am thanking them for. I think it's always a good idea to send a written thank-you. Never try to save a stamp.

"When someone does something for the University," Frohnmayer added, "we try to thank them within forty-eight hours. Every letter of that kind has a hand-written postscript from me. This is true whether we are sending five or five hundred."

Of course if you are going to offer praise, it is best to do so in the most powerful and resonant way possible. To that end we offer the following model, designed to help you to help others understand how appreciated they are. [see Figure 6-A on page 114]

Gratitude and Recognition
—Summary

1. **Look for opportunities for sincere praise.**

2. **Catch people doing things right.**

3. **Keep encouragement pure.**

4. **Focus on specific information.**

5. **Be a compliment messenger.**

6. **Praise in multiple directions.**

Figure 6-A

The Gratitude and Recognition Model

Step 1—Thank: Acknowledge someone's effort sincerely.

Step 2—Offer Specifics: Tell the person exactly what behaviors you found helpful or admirable. Be sure to mention the behaviors you'd most like to see repeated.

Step 3—Note Benefits: Enumerate the ways in which the person you are thanking created a positive outcome (for you, for the work group, for the family, etc.).

Step 4—Thank Again: End by reiterating, and thus reinforcing, how grateful you are. [see Figure 6-B on page 116]

This model represents the kind of praise sandwich we like. It is unambiguous. It includes nothing but the finest ingredients, inside and out. In whatever circumstance this model is employed, it will communicate gratitude and recognition with utmost clarity. Here are a few examples of how it can be used:

"Thank you so much for rescheduling your meeting so that I could attend. I didn't want to miss the last day of my conference. Enabling me to meet with our team afterward let me gather a lot of valuable information and then share it with them. I couldn't have pulled it off without your cooperation. I appreciate it."

"I'm so grateful to you for holding down the fort and looking after the kids while I went to visit my Mom. I realize you had to juggle your work schedule around and do double duty at home. Flying out to see Mom in the hospital really cheered her up, and I expect that will help her recover more quickly. Did I mention that you're a great husband and I love you?"

"Thanks for being so responsible about calling us when you knew you were going to be late getting in last night. Your mother and I would have been awfully worried if we hadn't known about the rain delay at the ball game. We're glad it all worked out, and, again, thanks for being considerate."

Thank - Specific - Benefit - Thank

1. Thank:

_____

_____

2. Specific:

_____

_____

3. Benefit:

_____

_____

4. Thank:

_____

_____

Figure 6-B

Remember, we're so biologically conditioned to focus on thorns in our side that offering detailed praise and recognition will feel awkward at first. However, this model is like all the others: The more frequently you use it, the easier it becomes. As with every other persuasive communication skill, you will move through stages of feeling more and more natural, until letting people know how much you value them becomes second nature.

The Positive Psychology of Gratitude

The value of expressing gratitude and recognition is supported by a groundbreaking body of research that stems from the burgeoning positive-psychology movement. Positive psychology is shifting the focus of psychology away from focusing on what causes neurosis and mental illness, toward a focus on what generates positive emotions and mental health. Studies that have emerged from this field show that improvements occur when, instead of focusing on "fixing" weaknesses, good traits that people already possess are encouraged and cultivated.[8]

Incorporating the acknowledgement—of people's creativity, diplomacy, compassion, generosity, humor, optimism, or determination—into our daily discourse is a profound problem-solving strategy. Gratitude and recognition enhance people's ability and willingness to draw on their strengths. It is always our strengths, ultimately, that help us in the face of adversity.

It's *Not* Nothing, It's Something

We're not quite done with the topic of expressing gratitude until we examine the other side of the coin. Just as most of us are not used to expressing gratitude, most of us are also not used to receiving it. To foster a culture where praise becomes a norm, we must make it acceptable to receive praise as well as to give it.

Have you ever noticed how difficult it is to graciously accept a compliment? Think about how you respond when someone says:

"You did a wonderful job."

"You are so thoughtful."

"You made me so happy."

"Your gift was perfect."

As much as we all like to hear these things, part of us flinches when we do. In fact, most of us are so resistant to taking in praise or gratitude that our response serves to dismiss and discourage the person who recognized us.

"You did a wonderful job."
"Oh, it was nothing."

"Your gift was perfect."
"Oh, don't mention it."

"You are so thoughtful."
"Oh, no big deal."

These figures of speech turn out to be universal. Thank someone in France and the reply will be *de rien*. In Spain it's *da nada*; in Greece, *tipota*; in Hungary, *semmi*. In every instance, the reply translates as *it's nothing*. What's more, these disclaimers are likely to be accompanied by body language consisting of a wave of the hand and an aversion of the eyes.

Do we really think our efforts were *nothing?* No. Do we really wish the person thanking us would stop? No. The truth is that although we're pleased to be praised, we're also embarrassed. But that's not because we're unduly humble; it's simply because no one ever taught us how to act in such a circumstance.

We're not suggesting you respond to a compliment with a boast (*Damn right, I did a wonderful job*), nor with a wheedle (*Hey, what else am I doing that you like?*). But to discourage someone who has offered recognition actually serves to punish them for their goodwill. Understandably, people don't want to feel rebuked for praising, and when this happens the likelihood that they will praise again diminishes. Thanks will grow in proportion to positive responses such as, "You're so welcome. I appreciate the acknowledgement." Like all communication, gratitude is a two-way street.

Chapter Seven

Hardwiring Teamwork:
The Power of Collaboration

"Never doubt that a small group of thoughtful, committed people can change the world. Indeed, it is the only thing that ever has."
—*Margaret Mead*

In our last chapter we mentioned the interdependency that exists among us all. The dynamic of interdependency is with us throughout our lives. Knowing how to get others to acknowledge this interdependency and collaborate effectively is a critical part of the skill set of any influential communicator. That's what this chapter is about.

Each of us is born into a team—a family. As our lives progress, we become members of innumerable groups and teams, from Little League to Boy and Girl Scouts, from fraternities to civic groups, from church groups to co-op boards and work groups. We're all familiar with the pitfalls of operating within group environments when communication breaks down. The dynamics become excruciating.

Learning the skills associated with effective team communication can enhance and enliven every aspect of the group process. Meetings

of all kinds will evolve from dreaded on-demand appearances to anticipated gatherings where everyone has a say. Family discussions will evolve
from drama to dialogue. The decisions that evolve from those meetings
and discussions will be sounder and stronger, and have the power of
unconditional support behind them. Increased energy will be available
for positive action plans, rather than drained by unresolved conflict and
the stress related to it.

Influential communicators within groups can be the force that
ignites all of this potent change. But it's important to remember that
effectively communicating in group settings is not about running the
show but rather, paradoxically, about shutting up and helping *everyone*
involved to participate and feel heard.

A Growing Interest in Teams

In recent years this mutual reliance has been increasingly acknowledged
in the workplace, as organizations have consistently brought more employees together in teams. The trend toward working in teams began
decades ago, and the fact that it's more widespread than ever shows that
it has far outlived "fad" status.

In March 2003, the World Health Organization (WHO) issued
a global warning about a frightening new disease: SARS. WHO then
initiated a global effort to uncover the disease's source. Eleven research
labs around the world were asked to work together in a "collaborative
multi-center research project." The labs shared their work and analyzed
results in daily teleconferences. A mere month after their collaboration
had begun, the labs were confident to announce their discovery of the
SARS virus (a.k.a. the corona virus). As James Surowiecki writes in
The Wisdom of Crowds, it might have taken any one of the labs years
to isolate the virus had they been working alone. Working together, it
took just a matter of weeks.

The success of the team approach results from several dynamics:

- **People support what they help create.** Zeal and commitment emanate from participation. When people have

input into a process, a product, or a decision, they are emotionally invested in it and will put tremendous energy into a positive outcome.

- **People closest to the work are in the best positions to make recommendations about it.** Teams comprised of individuals with differing responsibilities and areas of expertise ensure that all relevant perspectives are taken into account.

- **The whole is often greater than the sum of its parts.** Creative ideas grow exponentially via brainstorming and collaboration. Individuals' unique perceptions and points of view can synergize to produce remarkable end results that one person alone rarely could have achieved.

Teamwork and teambuilding—the process through which team members examine their behavior and design actions to improve the group's performance—are critical not only to the world of work, but also to community groups, volunteer organizations, team sports, and even to family life. However, effective teamwork is impossible without effective communication. Good communication is a factor in the successes of any team, while poor communication is nearly always cited as a factor when teams fail to meet their goals.

Hardwiring Effective Team Talk

Effective team functioning produces observable and measurable performance results. But performance only improves if teams are cooperating and collaborating. To simply create teams without exposing them to the skills they need to be effective is to give nothing more than a perfunctory nod to the team concept.

To examine how team dynamics can be improved, and what that would mean to how the team functioned, we undertook a three-year study of a fire management unit in the forests of the western United

States. We were called in as practitioner-clinicians to work with this team because its members were experiencing difficulties.[9]

The team consisted of twelve members of a management unit. When team members were initially interviewed, they all said that morale was at an all-time low. Charges of nepotism had created mistrust, as had the arrival of "fast-trackers" from outside the district who were viewed as self-interested careerists. In addition, a charge of sexual harassment had led to team polarization. There were low levels of trust, a high degree of divisiveness, and what team members referred to as "back-stabbing."

We initiated a series of retreats, devoted to team members learning skills and then applying those skills to develop team agreements. Applying these skills, they developed a series of agreement statements that transformed the communication practices of their team.

With each successive retreat, skills were reviewed and refined. Feedback to each member was provided by each of the others, and all participants evaluated how the group had changed. Three years following the first teambuilding retreat, follow-up interviews revealed perceptions of teamwork substantially different than before the interventions. Team members were committed to confronting problems and accepting criticism. Commitment to communication dominated when potential problems emerged. All agreed that no problem was so great they would let it interfere with their relationships. As one member observed, "Before, people only cared for themselves. Now, everyone is excited about each other's victories."

Team members undermining one another is only one dynamic that can seriously inhibit effectiveness. Things can also go wrong when members don't speak up within the group—either they don't contribute ideas or they don't ask the right questions—or when no one from the team communicates its decisions to others who need to know outside the team.

In an earlier chapter, we mentioned communication issues that contributed to NASA's two shuttle disasters. NASA's failed 1999 mission, in which a $125-million Mars Orbiter was lost, offers another such example—illustrating how teamwork and effective communication failed to coincide, with disastrous results.

In this instance, the space agency's team worked out its equations for a key spacecraft operation using the metric system (a system it had been using for years). Meanwhile, an outside vendor's engineering team applied English units of measurement. The mismatch of measurement standards prevented navigation information from transferring accurately between the Mars Climate Orbiter spacecraft team, in Denver, and the flight team at NASA's Jet Propulsion Laboratory, in Pasadena, California. A subsequent NASA review panel cited—no surprise—poor communication and teamwork across project elements among the key reasons for the mission's demise.[10] Mistakes happen, but had effective communication been built into the process, there's little doubt that the discrepancy would have been discovered in time to avoid such a failure.

Of course it's one thing to say that teams need better communication. It's quite another to make certain this occurs. In order for teams to function effectively, the members of those teams need to develop skills in communication, problem solving, and decision making.

Though a particular person may be designated team leader, little good will come from interpreting this title as license to boss the team around. Leaders of teams, however, do have a special responsibility. If they mean to exert a positive influence on the group process, they need to develop excellent collaborative skills, and also to model them for others.

The Influential Communicator as Catalyst

Even though most leaders have come to embrace the concept of teamwork, too many feel ill-equipped to develop true partnerships within organizations.

To be a collaborative leader is to be a catalyst. In scientific terms, a catalyst is a chemical that speeds up the rate of a chemical reaction, like an enzyme that quickens food digestion. In our context, it refers to a person who helps to make change happen.

Being a communication catalyst requires a special set of competencies:

1. **The ability to decide on the right level of participation for each decision**, and to be certain, before the discussion begins, that everyone is clear about who will make the decision.

2. **Group facilitation skills** to make meetings productive, action-packed, and safe, where a tremendous amount is accomplished and people feel committed to the results.

3. **A problem-solving approach** that is simple, complete, and can be learned by everyone in the organization, transforming people with differing opinions and perspectives into a collaborative force supporting an action agenda.

Let's examine each of these competencies one by one.

Setting a Decision Mode

Even in participative organizations, not all decisions are shared. Essentially, there are three decision-making types: command, consultive, and consensus. Any high-performance organization requires a range of all three.

In *command decisions,* the leader calls the shot: "This company is going to be taken public."

LEADER > >>>>>>>> GROUP

In *consultive decisions*, the leader makes the decision with input, ideas, and insights from the group: "The idea of taking this company public is under consideration. Before I make my decision I want you all to offer your thoughts on the matter."

LEADER > <<<<<<<< GROUP

In *consensus decisions*, the leader's opinions carry no more weight than anyone else's: "Whether or not this company goes public will depend on what the group as a whole determines."

LEADER <<<<<>>>>> GROUP
[see Figure 7-A on page 128]

Persuasive communicators in high-performance organizations are comfortable moving back and forth from one mode to another. They understand why and when each mode must be present.

If all decisions come from the top, there's a danger that problem detection from the rank and file will go unheeded (remember those "O" ring seals). There's also a high probability that the organization will lack creativity, and that employees will rightfully believe that their experience and input are not valued.

If all decisions are consultive, with the leader still making the final call even after group input, group members may become resentful. They will feel that no one actually listens to their ideas and that, although they are being asked for an opinion, minds are already made up. Finally, they'll grow tired of these resentments and bring their input to a halt.

If all decisions are consensus, employees can become bored and tired of countless meetings to decide trivial matters.

Most common pitfalls can be avoided if leaders give the choice of decision mode the thorough and careful consideration it deserves. Many factors enter into the selection of a decision mode, including who the stakeholders are in the outcome and its implementation, who has valuable information to offer, and whether or not insight from group members could be potent enough to tip the scale. Leader Insight 7-1 on page 129 provides an example of how a skillful leader makes a command decision acceptable to a resistant group of medical providers.

Command Decisions

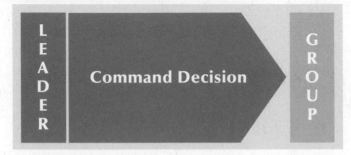

Leader calls it.

Consultive Decisions

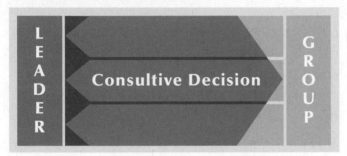

Leader makes the decision with input, ideas, insights from group.

Consensus Decisions

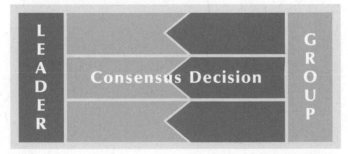

Leader's voice is no stronger than anyone else's.

Figure 7-A

Leader Insight 7-1

A Command Decision Helps Consensus—and Change—Evolve

When Peace Health System, a group of hospitals and healthcare facilities in Oregon, Washington, and Alaska, wanted to implement advanced information technology systems that would enhance the quality and safety of patient care, John Haughom, M.D., was brought in to lead the information services group. Haughom describes the transition process he oversaw as nothing less than a complete cultural transformation.

"The technology we implemented was enormously complex, but that was a tiny fraction of the challenge," says Haughom. "The challenge was on the people side. Being able to change the culture from where it was to where it needed to be meant getting people to embrace massive changes."

Haughom's mission included moving the healthcare organization from a paper-based to a completely paperless digital world—a change with impact on virtually every daily process. "The goal was to improve communication and information exchange," Haughom explained, "but it would not work unless we persuaded the people involved to get behind that goal and see the promise."

Although the decision to implement the new technology had been, in essence, a command decision, Haughom noted, "Command decision makers have to communicate their vision. Ultimately, you have to be extremely good at communicating so people understand why they will benefit from going from where they are to a new place, and what processes will be involved. The communication needs to be such that they *want* to be involved."

The people most impacted by the changes were medical staffers—doctors, nurses, pharmacists, lab technicians—with little knowledge of computers. "There was enormous resistance," recalled Haughom. "Many people said this was a boondoggle, the worst thing that ever happened to them. Some even threatened to boycott."

Realizing that the fears and complaints had to be addressed, Haughom and his team launched a communication campaign. "We kept putting out the message of why we were doing this—that better access to information would increase quality of care and safety. Even though some people didn't believe it, they kept hearing it and kept learning it. It was a consistent message about where we were going and why we were going there.

"Another part of our effort was extensive training and education to help people feel comfortable with this new reality," Haughom continued. "A big piece of this—and I used to get kidded about it, but it worked—was that each time we had even the smallest success, we would trumpet it and celebrate it. Because of this we started getting more and more feedback on success stories. A physician would realize he could instantly access the records of a patient being transferred to his hospital for surgery and he would send a happy email and say, 'I get it.'

"Finally," said Haughom, "we had four analysts conducting ongoing meeting sessions where we listened to their grievances and frustrations. These analysts' full-time jobs were to listen and understand. Frustrations were always seen as legitimate. We heard people's concerns and learned to weave what they needed into what we created. If you listen to people's frustrations, you can usually find a way to build that concern into forward progress—and give people a sense of ownership."

As time went on, the successes got bigger and bigger. One measure of success, Haughom said, was when new and different ideas were so widely accepted that they spawned a common vocabulary. "I would go to a meeting with some of the physicians who had previously been some of the biggest thorns in my side. They had been totally anti-technology. Now we were speaking the same language, using the same terms." A pleased Haughom kept his sense of triumph to himself. "I didn't point out that there had been a paradigm shift," he said. " I kept my mouth shut."

Group Facilitation Skills

When a choice to seek consensus is made, the opportunity is powerful and the challenge great. As anyone who has ever been in a meeting would surely agree, high-performance meetings are rare. (According to a *USA Today* survey, 54 percent of U.S. workers would rather mow the lawn than go to an office meeting, 25 percent would rather visit the dentist, and 23 percent would rather read the phone book.)

The participative leader is able to help a group navigate through a dialogue, craft decisions, and resolve difficult issues. The leader must not only be a catalyst to facilitate action, but also must empower and encourage everyone else to become a process facilitator. In meetings where consensus is the desired outcome, all group members should become *participant observers*—offering opinions and, at the same time, being entrusted to keep an eye on the very process that enables everyone to have a say.

But how can a participative leader get grandstanders to stop hogging the floor and encourage the would-be invisible people to take a stand? The answer lies in a balanced blend of *task skills* and *relationship skills*. Task skills are about accomplishing the group's goal efficiently: getting the work completed, the decision made, and the problem solved in record time. Relationship skills ensure that the emotional climate is safe, that everyone participates, that people feel heard and understood, and that all feel positive about the process and, most importantly, committed to its results.

Task Skills

In an ideal consensus-driven situation, everyone in the group is given—and takes—a turn to speak. But this is difficult to accomplish without a commitment to discipline, brevity, and clarity. Rambling on and on in a group setting takes valuable time away from others and decreases the odds that everyone will have a chance—let alone a desire—to contribute. Following are some key task-oriented skills geared to enable efficient input into a group.

Using P.R.E.S.—Point, Reason, Example, Summary

Regardless of what subject is up for discussion, P.R.E.S. is the most powerful way to get quickly to the heart of the matter. Begin your statement with the main point you wish to communicate; substantiate your idea with a reason; offer an example of what you mean; briefly sum up your thoughts.

"I believe we should resist taking this company public for the time being. Taking it public would make us too focused on quarter-by-quarter profits in order to please investors. Many in our industry rushed to go public during the dot.com craze and lost sight of their long-term goals. I think the matter should be put on hold until a later date."

"I think going public now would benefit us as an organization. The influx of capital would let us make great headway with research and development. One of our competitors has recently gone public and now has an advantage in this area. In my opinion, the time to move is now."

Asking questions

Whenever we observe groups, we notice that while opinions are common, questions are rare. Asking questions lets important information surface and allows people to feel heard and understood.

Polling

Check periodically to determine the level of agreement. ("So how many people think we should go forward?") Then ask the dissenters to clarify their concerns.

Summarizing

Keep track of the discussion by periodically segmenting off agreement and then focusing on the precise points of clash remaining to be resolved. ("I believe we all agree on at least three points. Here are two points of disagreement we still need to resolve.") The ability to summarize is a hallmark of persuasive communicators. Studies on emergent leadership suggest that the person who tends to emerge as the prime influencer in a group of leaders is the person who is able to summarize by capturing agreements and keeping the group focused on resolving the precise clash points that remain.

Using the 80/20 principle

Find the 20 percent of the discussion that captures 80 percent of the results. Call 80/20 when you believe the discussion has reached a point of diminishing returns, when people are repeating themselves without adding any new information.

Relationship Skills

Task skills are about economy of action and about working smart. They are necessary but not sufficient for catalyzing a group. Group members must also feel secure enough to speak up, safe enough to disagree, and absolutely committed to the decision that emerges from the group. Once the participative leader embraces and models relationship skills, others will begin to do so themselves. The entire group will become emotion-ally intelligent facilitators. Following are some key relationship-oriented skills.

- **Speaking for yourself.** When offering an observation or opinion, speak in the first person. ("Here's what I've noticed…what I believe…how I feel.") "I" language is accountable, whereas "you" language can sound accusa-tory, and talking in the royal "we" can sound presump-tuous and be inaccurate. *(We're unhappy with company benefits.)*

- **Listening actively.** Display nonverbal curiosity with your body language and facial expressions. (Lean in; make eye contact; nod when you agree.) Verbally show that you are paying attention by paraphrasing, especially before you disagree or challenge another's opinion.

- **Gatekeeping.** Invite quieter people into the conversa-tion. Make it clear that the group *needs* their ideas. A reticence to speak does *not* equate to having nothing to contribute. These are exactly the group members who may hold the key to consensus. Still waters run deep.

- **Complimenting and agreeing.** It's important to make agreement obvious. ("Good idea. I hadn't thought about that before.") When group members realize they are influ-encing each other, energy and momentum soar. Agreeing and complimenting will alter the group's biochemistry for the better, and encourage even more participation.

- **Using humor.** Sharing a laugh with others is a wonder-ful bonding experience. Joint laughter allows a group to feel safe and unified. Naturally, a laugh at the expense of a group member can be alienating. Persuasive communi-cators are at ease laughing about themselves.

- **Process checking.** If the process isn't working, take time out to fix it. If a few people are dominating, if some haven't spoken at all, if someone engages in a sarcastic tirade, call for a process check and address the situation. It's not possible to solve complex problems effectively with a process that's not working.

- **Building a written consensus.** Consensus doesn't just happen; it must be constructed. In order to achieve this, persuasive communicators are writing down sound bytes of agreement as they evolve. This is counter-intuitive, since most people engage in group discussions by listening for holes in the argument. Here we focus on the threads of common ground that can be woven together. When consensus is in writing, everyone understands exactly what's being agreed to.

- **Final process checking.** In this concluding skill, all group members comment on how they evaluated the meeting. Each person gets 30 seconds to think and 20 seconds to tell the group how he or she experienced the meeting. This allows for psychological closure and improvements in subsequent meetings.

Building consensus is the most sophisticated skill we teach, because it requires so many different abilities. But the value of constructing a true consensus in a group is so powerful that it is worth every bit of effort. In addition, even though this model initially grew out of our work with business, government, and nonprofit organizations, we've come to see over the years how effective a strategy of consensus building can be within all sorts of groups, not the least of which is families.

Just as in other groups, family leaders (a.k.a. fathers and mothers) can determine which decisions are the command type, which are consultive, and which are consensus. A decision about, say, how much the family can afford to spend on a vacation would almost certainly be made at the command level; nevertheless, a choice of destinations may well merit a consensus. (If you don't believe us, try taking your teenagers to a spot they don't want to go and see what a grand time you all have together.)

Family structures have been traditionally hierarchical, with parents calling the shots and children doing as they're told—or arguing relentlessly for input. Many of us did not grow up in homes where consensus building was the norm, but think how much more skillful we would be if we had. Now imagine how well we can prepare our children for the future by training them to think collaboratively and by giving them the tools they need to do so.

A Model for Collaborative Problem Solving

The final model we're going to provide in this chapter is a potent technique for creating solutions to open-ended problems and ongoing challenges. It allows groups to brainstorm in the most inventive and productive manner possible. Where *ad hoc* brainstorming can often turn into a free-for-all, with group members going off on their own tangent, our model for collaborative problem solving offers a road map and a structure that is simple, thorough, and action oriented—and that drives through to results.

The model begins with an open-ended question: "What steps can we take to improve our service to customers?"

> *"What can we do to achieve better coordination and cooperation across departments in our organization?"*

> *"What measures can we take to enhance safety practices among our workforce?"*

For optimal results, the question should always be phrased in a positive manner. A growing body of research in an area known as *appreciative inquiry* has revealed that phrasing questions positively ("What three wishes do you have for this company?") rather than negatively ("What's wrong with this company?") rejuvenates the thought processes.[11] As an example, a national airline successfully addressed a late baggage issue when it stopped asking how to fix the late baggage problem and stimulated stakeholders by asking, "What can we do to create an exceptional arrival experience for our customers?"

Such an approach transforms traditional problem solving into a high-energy exploration of what is working and of how to strengthen the group's positive core. People are naturally enthusiastic when they participate in a collaborative process aimed at acknowledging and enhancing the conditions that are present when they are performing at their best. Group synergy is maximized when people are asked to focus on achievements, strengths, opportunities, and shared visions of potential futures that will be valued by one and all.

From a technical standpoint, three additional elements will need to be in place. The first is a flip chart that serves as the **group memory**. Ideas jotted down on the chart belong to the group as a whole. They are noted by a **facilitator/recorder** whose function it is to keep track of ideas while maintaining the process. Finally, **horseshoe seating** should be arranged, with all participants having the group memory chart in full view.

Now the process can begin.

Step 1: Silent Brainstorming

- Allow two silent minutes for individuals to reflect on the question—in writing.
- Think big; think small. The important thing is to come up with a quantity of ideas.
- Do *not* be constrained by convention, cost, or what's happened before.

Step 2: Round Robin Input

- The facilitator/recorder solicits one item at a time from each person.
- Items are numbered as they are put into group memory.
- No evaluations or blocking statements (including non-verbal blockers such as eye-rolling) are allowed.

- Questions for clarification are allowed, with brief responses.
- Should members temporarily run out of ideas, they simply say "pass" on their turn. People can reclaim their turn after passing.

Step 3: Discuss and Advocate

- Everyone speaks.
- Everyone listens.
- Everyone feels heard and understood.
- Members advocate positions based on two criteria: 1) the impact the idea would have on the problem; 2) how doable is the idea and can the group make it happen? Evaluating an idea's plausibility must address whether its results can be observed and measured. You can't manage it if you can't measure it.
- Members should be persuasive (remember the P.R.E.S. model) but still open to others' ideas.
- After the discussion is complete, members can cluster items that address the same idea. Avoid mega-clusters.

Step 4: Prioritize

- Considering all you've heard, assign values to ideas:
    Three points—top choice
    Two points—second choice
    One point—third choice
- First, people assign values individually in writing.
- Recorder notes down all three-, two-, and one-point values.
- Scores are added to determine top-ranked ideas.

Step 5: Choosing Champions

- Starting with top-ranked items, ask two people to volunteer as champions for each high-priority action.
- The champion is not the doer, but rather the group conscience—keeping the action on the group's front burner.
- Getting the group to move into action fosters a joint identity as "a group that makes things happen."

[see Figure 7-B on page 140]

Each of these five steps allows people from various parts of the organization, all with differing thoughts and opinions—to come together and drive through to solutions. The first step is designed to break through resistance to creativity and spontaneity. It should take just enough time to get the creative juices flowing. The second step is crafted to encourage universal participation. By the third step, the ideas are beginning to take on a distinctive shape, becoming more refined and more realistic and merging with compatible concepts. By the fourth step, clear choices emerge. By the fifth step, those ideas have genuine impetus and enthusiasm behind them.

Some people have a harder time than others using persuasive communication skills in group settings. Group dynamics can be complex. Hearing from everyone and achieving consensus take time. It's often tempting to "move it along" and "wrap it up." If a group member isn't speaking, it's all too easy to assume he or she has nothing to say. But here's a story we heard from a seminar alumnus who runs a nonprofit foundation that offers mental health services to residents of a large city. It illustrates why inclusion and listening pay off:

> "I was running a board meeting where there were a number of sensitive issues on the table. Our funding had been cut by the state once again and we needed to

A Model for Collaborative Problem Solving—Summary

STEP 1 Silent Brainstorming

STEP 2 Round Robin Input

STEP 3 Discuss and Advocate

STEP 4 Prioritize

STEP 5 Choose Champions

Allows people to come together from all parts
of the organization, with differing ideas and opinions,
in a collaborative partnership to solve difficult problems
and drive through to results.

Figure 7-B

make cutbacks while generating new ideas for fundraising. The meeting dragged on, and I noticed one board member who looked like he was napping. I couldn't say I blamed him, but still I felt annoyed. Finally, I decided to see what would happen if I included him. I called his name and asked him if he had any ideas about how to meet our challenges. He immediately sprang to life and contributed about half a dozen of the best ideas we'd heard all evening. I now see that still waters run deep, and I've vowed to always ask all group members to contribute their thoughts."

Remember, it is perfectly normal to feel phony and uncomfortable in the early stages of any new communication behavior. But each time a group member who might have remained silent makes a valuable contribution, you—as the persuasive communicator who served as the catalyst—will feel reinforced. Soon, you will be in the habit of reaching out to all group members. The behavior will feel so comfortable it will become second nature. Leader Insight 7-2 provides a glimpse of a successful collaborative process.

Leader Insight 7-2

Collaboration of a Mass Scale: The Chalkboard Project

"We started with agreement. We agreed there were problems with Oregon public education," said Norm Smith, President of the Ford Family Foundation and one of the coordinators of the Chalkboard Project. "But we assiduously avoided the $64,000 question: What should be done? We needed to find out what everyone was willing to do."

Smith is describing the genesis of a collaborative entity—the Chalkboard Project—that has been operating since 2002 to engage hundreds of thousands of Oregonians, from the state's six diverse regions, on the topic of creating a quality, accountable, and stably funded public education system.

Oregon's education challenges are myriad, or as Smith puts it, "on the scope of world hunger." Quality and test scores have been declining, as has confidence in the system. Debt has severely escalated, and school attendance numbers are among the poorest in the country. Among the public, expectations and opinions have been plentiful and varied, but solutions have proved elusive. What was needed was consensus.

To drive that consensus, five organizations—The Ford Family Foundation, the Collins Foundation, the JELD-WEN Foundation, the Meyer Memorial Trust, and the Oregon Community Foundation—joined together. "It all began with directors from each of these groups sitting around saying 'What if?'," said Smith. The collaboration was ultimately formalized and funded with a quarter-million-dollar grant from each of the five groups.

"Some of the five groups are more conservative, some more liberal," said Smith. "Some are rurally focused, some more urban. Four are private and one, the Oregon Community Foundation, is public. Each has its own very different leadership and rules of governance. We had never collaborated before, but we came together like a bunch of one-celled organisms evolving into a multi-celled animal.

"The group's first task was to undertake more public-opinion polling than had ever been done," said Smith. Extensive sampling from all across the state monitored people's standing on the issues and indicated that up to a third of all Oregonians might be willing to engage in a project of this scale.

"On the heels of launching the polling," Smith continued, "we initiated a research operation by a cadre of educational scholars, who generated reports on best practices internationally, nationally, and locally. This is when we discovered some startling anomalies about Oregon, such as our extraordinarily low student-attendance numbers. The research portion of Chalkboard is bolstered by an outer circle of regional and national experts who peer-review our data and ask clarifying questions."

What Chalkboard has done is nothing less than create multiple, overlapping collaborations—of organizations, of scholars, and, most significantly, of vast numbers of citizens. Smith says one critical element in all this is the collaboration between the five founding organizations. "If we five groups are not linked arm in arm—even though we may philosophically disagree," he says, "we will fail." An additional key, says Smith, "is that we have a uniform way of engaging people with very diverse demographics. We are getting participation from parents, students, school administrators, and state agencies."

As for long-term goals, Smith says: "We are looking at the realm of public policy change, major systemic change. First, we want to establish what the biases are. Then we want to replace those biases with facts. Then we want to cut back toward consensus. The reason we can accomplish what others have tried to accomplish is that we are viewed as—and are—neutral. What we contributed was the process, not the outcome."

Chapter Eight

Using The Juice:

Public Speaking and the Motor of Anxiety

When our son, Sam, was in the second grade, he came home from school one day sporting the telltale clean-tracks-across-a-dirty-face look of a boy who'd been crying. We coaxed out of him the fact that he and a classmate had fumbled a class presentation, which now required a "do over" for tomorrow. Sam confided that during the presentation his heart had been "beating so hard that everyone saw my shirt moving." The thought of a repeat performance was too much to bear.

The agony Sam was going through was all too familiar. During our graduate work at Penn State, we worked with clinically apprehensive, painfully shy students for five years. Like the many people with whom we had worked in the shyness clinics early in our career, Sam had become a prisoner of his own physiological, mental, and emotional responses. Having made a failed attempt to address an audience with calm and clarity, Sam was now frightened of his fear itself.

We reassured Sam that he was, in fact, fully prepared for the next day, that he had everything he needed to give a great talk. We told him that the fearful feeling he had experienced was actually "the juice." Juice, we explained, was what the body provided as fuel for facing an audience. It meant you were alert, centered, prepared for anything.

Later that night we overheard Sam talking to his copresenter on the phone. "Matt, we weren't scared," he said. "My parents said we just had 'the juice,' and if we have it again tomorrow we'll be great."

Sam is a junior at Berkeley now, and still a devotee of the juice. So are thousands of people around the country whom we have urged to reframe anxiety—the physical signs of which so closely mirror those of positive excitement—as a force for dynamic delivery and powerful persuasion.

An Unspeakable Terror

No matter how skillful one may be when communicating one-on-one, or even in small group settings, there's a high probability that addressing an audience will strike terror in the heart. In surveys of common fears by Bruskin & Associates, many people actually rank their fear of public speaking as higher than their fear of death (!).[12] Yet to a rare few people, public speaking seems to come effortlessly. They are able to hold an audience enthralled while exciting and inspiring its members.

But were these naturals always so natural? In many cases, no. Mahatma Gandhi fainted from sheer anxiety the first time he presented a court case as a young lawyer. An extraordinary number of entertainers, including Barbra Streisand, Bob Hope, Carol Burnett, and Carly Simon, have spoken of stage fright so acute it kept them from performing. What did these "naturals" have to learn? Obviously they've mastered the physical dynamics of facing an audience, using voice cadence and body language to maximum effect. Gandhi, of course, learned to craft a message in such a powerful way as to motivate millions. But before they could do any of that, they had to come to terms with their anxiety.

This chapter will teach you to harness and utilize anxiety to make your public communication more persuasive than you ever thought possible.

It may seem paradoxical to imagine capitalizing on anxiety. Most of us think of our apprehension as something to be eradicated. Those sweaty palms, that rapid heartbeat and shallow breath, that flushed face and those trembling extremities—if we could banish these symptoms we'd be fine, right?

Wrong. These hallmarks of anxiety are identical to the hallmarks of enthusiastic anticipation and even exhilaration. It's our *perception and labeling* of our sensations that matters. Anxiety's stranglehold occurs only when we label it as something to be feared and avoided. It is this secondary fear that can devastate performance.

Principles for Harnessing Anxiety

Attempting to suppress anxiety is futile. Even if you could do so, it would prove counter-productive. The world's most dynamic and charismatic speakers realize that anxiety is the motor of performance. Thus, the five principles offered here are *not* meant to fend off anxiety but, paradoxically, to help you welcome it and optimize its power.

1. **Embrace anxiety; don't fear it.** Become aware of your self-talk. When you feel that butterfly-in-the-stomach reaction, say to yourself, "This is the juice, the motor of performance. I embrace it; I'm glad it's here with me."

2. **Control nonverbal cues that signal anxiety.** Ask: What do I look like when I'm enthusiastic and in control? (For example: I look right at people; my voice modulates naturally; I place my hand casually in my pocket.) Ask: What do I look like when "I'm 'losing it'?" (For example: I look at the ground; I speak in a monotone or hear my

voice break; I stiffen up.) Now, no matter how you feel, perform the actions you would perform when you experience yourself as in control. *It's easier to act yourself into new ways of feeling than to feel yourself into new ways of acting.*

3. **Maximize eye contact.** Whether there are 20, 200, or 2000 people in the room, talk only to one person at a time. Look first at the people who seem the most interested. They will keep you clear and focused. As you harness anxiety, make eye contact with those who seem more removed. Your fervor and confidence will draw them in.

4. **Practice and rehearse in your mind.** Using an outline, practice in your mind several times, challenging yourself to use different words each time. Know your material thoroughly so you can improvise and embellish. Visualize yourself performing well. Successful imaginary rehearsal correlates with successful performance.

5. **Prepare for going blank.** All speakers lose their train of thought at some point. Anticipate it as a routine event. When you draw a blank, act as if you are okay. Say, "Let me be sure I've covered everything." Return to your notes and then say, "Oh, yes, one more thing…"

Each of these five principles is part of an inoculation—not against fear, but against the fear of fear. Start off by accepting—even welcoming—anxiety as the fundamental key. That attitude is bolstered by action. Regardless of how you feel, act the way you act when you are invigorated—on top of the situation. Gaining control of your physical reactions to anxiety will redirect that anxiety toward a positive end. Be especially alert to the cue of stiffness in both voice and body language.

We tend to think of nervous people as fidgety, but in front of a group most nervous speakers actually become rigid and rote.

Another important physical strategy is to single out one audience member at a time for direct eye contact. Doing so transforms the feeling of facing a roomful of potential critics into that of talking to an engrossed and encouraging fan. And remember to choose people, at least initially, whose demeanor gives you confidence and energy.

Practicing and visualizing your message beforehand is especially useful in building confidence—not only because you will feel less need to rely on notes but also because the more you know your basic message, the more free you will be to spontaneously adapt to your audience. This kind of in-the-moment creativity can bring a speaker to the artful level of a great jazz musician doing a riff on a familiar piece while the audience listens spellbound.

Finally, embracing anxiety means being fully open to what many think of as the worst-case scenario. Simply assume you will lose your focus at some point—you are only human, after all. Just be prepared with a strategy to deal with it, and the potential panic attached to it will dissolve.

Eliminating Tentative Language Patterns

Another way to harness anxiety is to become aware of five language patterns that serve to make speakers appear tentative or anxious in the eyes of an audience. Over the years, we have noticed people unintentionally falling into patterns that signal uncertainty, tentativeness, and lack of commitment. We urge you to become aware of any tendency you may have to engage in these:

- **Tag questions** are statements that end in a question. Tag questions allow otherwise powerful statements to appear tentative and hesitant. Consider which of these is more powerful: "I think we should revamp the performance review system, do you?" "The performance review system needs to be revamped."

- **Qualifiers** are words that diminish your message: *sort of, kind of, maybe.* Would you feel motivated by "I'm sort of thinking that maybe we could kind of work together to…"?

- **Disclaimers** come at the beginning of statements. They signal our anxiety by implying, *Don't take me too seriously, because I lack confidence in myself.* Imagine yourself as a member of an audience. Would the following galvanize you? "I know a lot of you have more experience than I do, but I was thinking that possibly…"

- **Lengthened requests** come off sounding apologetic. They also serve to cancel themselves out by providing listeners with ample rationale not to pay attention to the request itself. Imagine how inspired to action you would be if someone said this to you: "I know you're awfully busy, and I'm probably not the most well-versed person in the field to be saying this, but I was thinking it might be a good idea to take a look at the performance review system."

- **Fillers and disfluencies** slow down the meaningful flow of language. They are words such as *um, er, you know, like.* They make the listener uncomfortable not only because they make a message sound disjointed, but also because their insertion serves to imply that the speaker doesn't know what comes next. As a rule, don't speak until you know what your next word will be. There is nothing wrong with a moment of silence. It builds anticipation, signals thoughtfulness, and is far preferable to stalling with babble.

The first step in purging your speech of tentative language patterns is to notice them. If you frequently use tag questions, qualifiers, or lengthened requests, you may have started doing so out of deference, or out of insecurity about the validity of your point of view when you were less experienced than you are now. The longer you went on using them, the more they became ingrained—and the more forcefully they worked against you.

Of all five tentative patterns, we've found that the one hardest to self-monitor and to self-correct is the tendency to use fillers and disfluencies. Since these often slip out without our knowing it, it's helpful to ask someone you trust to help you keep tabs on this tendency. We once worked with someone who had a friend ring a bell whenever an *um* or *er* came along in her conversation. And we ourselves helped our then teen-aged daughter notice her "you know" pattern by responding each time with, "Yes, Meegan, we know."

Doing away with tentative language patterns won't happen overnight, but the effort to address them is well worth it. As they gradually dissipate, you'll find yourself increasingly able to redirect your underlying anxiety and access the all-important juice that will help you transform your fear into infectious enthusiasm.

Chapter Nine

It's All About the Audience:
Delivering Persuasive Messages

Oratory is the oldest human art form. Throughout history it has been a vital means of motivating groups of people. Eloquent speech was highly valued in ancient India and China, as well as in the pre-Columbian cultures of North and South America. In 2500 B.C., a work known as *The Maxims of Ptah-hotep* gave advice to ordinary people (nearly all of them unable to write) who used oral argument to plead their cases and causes before official magistrates who delivered a verdict. (Ptah-hotep's counsel, by the way, discouraged angry and quarrelsome discourse and stressed the wisdom of self-control, humility, and knowing when to keep silent.)[13]

In classical Greece and Rome, oratory played a pivotal role in all of public life. And, of course, people still read Aristotle's *Rhetoric*, written in 350 B.C. Even prior to recorded history, groups were undoubtedly inspired by individuals who combined a command of language with personal charisma and influence.

Embracing anxiety is an essential first step to delivering messages that perpetuate the ancient art of convincing, exciting, and inciting listeners to action. However, harnessing anxiety is only part of persuasive public speaking. The steps we discuss in this chapter are also essential. They encompass the skills of crafting influential messages and delivering them in ways that are irresistibly compelling. It is important to keep in mind that these skills apply whether we're speaking to an audience of 500 in a conference hall or five people in a meeting.

As we present strategies for persuasive speech, we'll be drawing on lessons learned from history's rhetorical masters and also on the knowledge gleaned from a large number of controlled experiments that, since the 1960s, have studied the variables that affect a speaker's impact.

But first, let's take a moment to get to the heart of an important underlying principle known to every world-class orator: *The secret of reaching an audience lies within the audience itself.*

Being Audience-Centric

Now would be a good time to revisit the title of this book, *Be Quiet, Be Heard.* When you make a presentation, you want to be heard. Still, it is absolutely imperative that you give paramount consideration to your listeners. The influential speaker untangling the persuasion paradox must always be aware of what the audience needs in order to absorb and accept the message.

The audience is the reason that the speaker is speaking. The audience is the judge of what transpires. Every aspect of the speaker's performance must be guided by the desire for the well being of the audience—and every audience member must sense that this is the case. As William Glasser writes, "People don't care what you know until they know you care."

As you begin to formulate what you wish to convey to your listeners, ask yourself these questions: *Who cares?* Why should the audience be concerned about my information? What benefits will it bring them? How will it help them to make their life easier, more productive, more enjoyable? How will it affect issues that concern them the most? Whenever you feel yourself falter, go off on a tangent, or otherwise lose your focus, this line of questioning will recenter you. Remember, if messages are not relevantly linked to the lives of the audience, listeners will disappear faster than a bowl of corn chips on Superbowl Sunday.

Speakers have no business speaking just to hear themselves. If they are speaking for self-glorification or simply performing for a fee, the audience will sense it in a heartbeat. What's more, if the audience changes, the message must be adapted. Never recycle the same content to groups with differing interests and concerns. This doesn't mean speakers must change their beliefs. It simply means that everything can—and should—be said in such a way as to be heard.

Tailoring a message to suit an audience requires using a full range of persuasive modes: *ethos*, *pathos*, and *logos*. *Ethos* refers to the credibility of the speaker. *Pathos* refers to the emotions the speaker is able to generate in the audience. *Logos* is the reason, logic, and argument of the presentation.

Aristotle said, "Rhetoric is the art of discovering, in any given case, all the available means of persuasion." Let's examine, one by one, the strategies by which an influential speaker can seamlessly weave all three together.

Ethos: Establishing Credibility

Aristotle believed that establishing credibility is based on the audience's perception of three characteristics: intelligence, character, and good will.

Establishing expertise certainly doesn't mean rattling off a list of your credentials, or sounding so cocky that everyone wonders why such a "big shot" would have time to speak to them. Establishing common ground with audience members goes a long way toward establishing credibility. They want to know that your core values are consistent with theirs—even if the specifics of what you have to say ultimately challenge some of their beliefs.

At the start of a speech, the audience wants to know about your character. Why do you care about what you're talking about? What compelled you to pursue it? If listeners know why and how much you care, then they begin to care about you and to sense that you are capable of caring about them as well.

Establishing credentials can often effectively be accomplished by personal anecdote. The question everyone wants to ask a renowned entomologist is most likely, "What on earth got you so interested in bugs?" A question for an astronaut: "What's it really like out there?" For a novelist: "Where do you come up with these characters?" Telling the audience what it is about your own topic that hooks and drives you serves a dual purpose. It explains why you became an expert and it begins to generate an infectious enthusiasm in audience members.

It's also important to remember that everything a speaker does throughout the course of a speech contributes to or detracts from initial credibility. To maintain your credibility, avoid two common pitfalls. Don't become a glorified guide to your own visuals. The audience came to see you, not a PowerPoint™ presentation. Also, don't read or memorize your remarks. No matter how stunning your visuals or how eloquent your writing, depending upon these tools does little to establish your authority and energy as a speaker.

Pathos: Inciting Emotion

Pathos moves beyond credibility into the realm of emotion. Knowing a great deal about a topic is one thing, but getting others to share your enthusiasm or conviction is quite another. Doubtless all of us have spent some time in our lives—perhaps too much time—listening to esteemed professors and highly credentialed experts who, although renowned for their brilliance, were dull as dishwater in their presentation. We recall very little of the material they were attempting to impart. It's the teachers and experts whose presentations were dynamic, and who were able to engage our emotions, who actually were able to share their knowledge with us. Here's what these dynamic speakers did right.

Create an appetite for the topic. If you want to feed a crowd and have them appreciate the fare, it's best to do so when they're hungry. Likewise, if you want your audience to appreciate what you have to say, you will need to create an *exigence*—an appetite, an urgency—for your topic.

You want your audience to understand that your message is central to their lives. You also want them to feel that *now is the time* for them to have and to use the knowledge you'll impart.

In order to create this situational urgency, you must be able to operate on the same frequency as your listeners. They want to know *what's in it for me*. That's a fair question, and one you must have uppermost in your mind as you create a desire for your message.

Create memorable examples. This is without a doubt *the most important factor* in a dynamic presentation. We cannot say it too often or too emphatically: People pay attention to and remember stories.

Stories are the most listened-to content in *any* speech. The best kind of example is a mini-drama, complete with characters and a plot (if there's a plot twist, so much the better). The story must build to a conclusion. The listeners must *care* about what happens at the end.

Whatever point you're trying to make, put a human face on it. If you are talking about the homeless, incorporating a detailed example of a homeless family will be more salient than a more general commentary about the problem. If you are talking about the high cost of healthcare, talking about people who've lost their coverage—especially people *like the audience members themselves*—will bring your point home more forcefully. And if you want to inspire people, the tale of one true hero will be the greatest possible stimulus.

As speakers, we constantly battle two enemies: boredom and confusion. Memorable examples are our greatest assets in both of these battles.

Pathos and Delivery Variables

From everything we've told you so far, it's obvious that content, language, and form are critical to moving an audience. Another key element in generating emotion, however, has nothing to do with content *per se*. It's the manner in which the content is delivered.

Delivery is a powerful motivator. It influences on a deep subliminal level. Audiences are generally unaware that the way in which something is said is gaining a hold on them. When delivery is strong, they are simply caught up in the process, as if under a speaker's spell.

The four critical delivery variables are pitch, volume, rate, and movement. We'll discuss each of them individually, but the main thing to remember about delivery variables is that it's the *variability* that matters. If any of these elements remains too static, the result is a dull, unclear delivery.

Pitch

Pitch is the fluctuation of voice between high and low ranges. We often think of the word pitch in the musical sense. Pitch, for example, distinguishes the sound made at one end of the piano from the sound at the other. The faster sound waves vibrate, the higher the pitch. The slower they vibrate, the lower the pitch. Changes in pitch are known as inflection. If you ask a question, your inflection rises at the end of a sentence.

Pitch conveys emotion. It can indicate if we're pleased or displeased, happy, angry, or sad. If someone tells you a piece of good news and you respond *oh my*, you will likely do so in a high pitch; if the news is bad, you'll most likely utter that *oh my* in a much lower pitch. Pitch can also be used to indicate sincerity or sarcasm. Think about the different inflection you use when you say *thanks a lot* to someone holding a door open for you, versus how you might say the same to someone who lets a door slam in your face.

Although we instinctively change our pitch to suit our conversation, we rarely think about consciously altering pitch to enhance our own dynamism. That's too bad, because often when we stand up before a group, the variance in our pitch actually lessens, thereby becoming more monotonous.

The deliberate variance of pitch is a potent rhetorical device—and most of us have a far greater range of pitch than we imagine. To test this, push your tone to its lowest pitch and begin counting at the number one. Now raise your pitch with each number and go as high as you can.

Once you've convinced yourself your pitch can truly vary, go ahead and alter it. Make a speech into a tape recorder and consciously use pitch to accentuate the meaning of your words. For a short while, do this in a manner that seems exaggerated, so that you sound "outrageous" to yourself and feel that you would be embarrassed for anyone else to hear the tape. Now play the tape back to yourself. You will be amazed at how dynamic you sound. By training your ear in this fashion, you will learn how to vary your pitch for maximum emotional impact.

Volume

Volume has to do with the softness or loudness of your voice. Again, variation is the key to using volume as a dynamic tool. While you always need to speak loudly enough to be heard (watch the people in the back of the room to see if they are straining), don't make the mistake of starting out too loudly and leaving yourself nowhere to go.

Don't always make your most emphatic points in your loudest voice. Build to your key points by speaking loudly, and then consider getting quiet to make the point itself. This calls people's attention to your point and even gets them to physically lean in for the payoff.

Rate

Rate is the speed at which a person speaks. It can also be envisioned as the amount of space between one's words. Rate of speech varies among the population. In the United States, people generally speak at a rate of between 120 and 150 words per minute, though there are many exceptions (John F. Kennedy spoke at 180 words per minute).

Whether we are "fast talkers" or "slow talkers," most of us don't tend to vary our rate all that much. But in public speaking a consistent rate is boring—even if that rate is consistently rapid. Mix it up. Martin

Luther King began his "I Have a Dream" speech at a pace of 92 words per minute and finished at 145.[14] King, a master orator by any standard, obviously understood the variability principal.

Note that varying rate of speech doesn't mean simply starting slowly and speeding up. As persuasive speakers know, it's effective to build to a key point with a fast rate, then pause, and finally use a slower rate to make the point itself. "I…have…a…dream."

Inexperienced speakers tend to race through their remarks as if they are dying to get them over with. A pause is what they dread most. But imagine writing an essay that didn't include any new paragraphs. That is what a speech without a pause sounds like to the listener. The more accomplished you become, the more you will feel comfortable using pauses for dramatic effect. Be sure to incorporate and practice them as you rehearse.

Movement

The first rule of movement is: Move. Don't get yourself stuck behind a podium. Walk around and stop in front of different groups of listeners, making eye contact with one audience member at a time. Conversely, don't let yourself become a perpetual motion machine.

One movement to assiduously avoid is rocking. A seasick audience is not a receptive audience. We know someone who put a pebble in one of his shoes to serve as a warning of when he was in danger of making his audience queasy.

Another common movement dilemma is what to do with one's hands. Some people let their hands do all of the talking. If you're prone to excessive hand gestures, imagine yourself under water to slow your movements down. Also, while you're maintaining eye contact with individual audience members, pay attention to whether that person's eyes are fixated on your hands. If so, you will know it's time to rein in your hand motion.

Conversely, it won't do to leave your hands lying limply at your sides. This conveys a sense of lethargy and stiffness. Try one hand in your pocket, the other bent at the elbow. You can switch them for variety and move both hands on occasion.

When we do one-on-one executive coaching, we make videotapes of our clients' presentations. At first they're usually embarrassed to view the results. But as we work with them on delivery variables and continue to play back the tapes, they're elated to see the progress they've made.

Varying pitch, volume, rate, and movement can make nearly any content come alive. But, of course, without sound content at its core, that liveliness is "all sizzle and no steak." All of which brings us to the final mode of persuasion.

Logos: Evidence, Organization, and Cohesive Logic

When a speaker has credibility as an individual coupled with a dynamic delivery that engages the audience's emotions, persuasion is in process. However, scanty evidence or poorly organized remarks can ignite skepticism. On the other hand, a presentation that is rich with evidence, well organized, and well reasoned will turn your listeners' wish to believe into conviction.

Evidence

Evidence is the support you bring to your position. It consists of material used to bolster your points. Whenever you say something that could conceivably be called into question, evidence is your greatest ally. It's especially useful if your target audience tends to hold a different point of view than yours. Among the most compelling types of evidence are:

Examples. An illustration or case in point is particularly powerful because it not only supports your position but also simultaneously increases interest. (Remember, your audience wants to hear about real people.)

Statistics. Numerical data can be extremely *convincing,* but most people are sophisticated enough to know that statistics can be misleading. You may need more than one statistic to back up a point. Though some people demand statistics in order to be influenced, many are suspicious of them. This means it is important to indicate the source of your statistics, and to help the audience understand why the source is credible.

Statistics converted into analogies. A second problem with statistics is that they can become boring. One of the best ways to turn a boring statistic into something motivating and understandable is to convert it into an analogy. Analogies make an argument by comparing the unknown with the known. Here are some examples:

- American adults spend an average of 170 minutes a day watching television and movies—nine times more than they spend exercising. (Dr. Andrew Weil, *Self-Healing*)

- Americans spend an average of twelve years of their life (24x7x52x12) watching TV. The average father spends two and a half minutes a day talking with his kids. By the time children are six, they've spent more time watching TV than they'll spend in their entire life talking to their father. (University of Kansas study)

- Annually, Americans spend more money on fast food than they do on higher education. (Eric Schlosser, *Fast Food Nation*)

Testimony, especially from unexpected sources. Identifying credible sources who advocate your position can be very persuasive. The gold standard of testimony comes from authority. An unexpected source: someone who the audience does not anticipate would be supporting your position. Here are some examples:

- When the actor who played the Marlboro man was dying of cancer, he became a spokesperson against the tobacco industry.

- In the days leading up to Richard Nixon's resignation, numerous Democrats called on the president to step down. It was when conservative Republican Barry Goldwater spoke out for the resignation that everything turned.

Residual Messages

What is the thing you most want your audience to remember when you are done speaking? This is known as your residual message. It's imperative that you decide ahead of time what you want this "take-away" to be.

Retention studies show that people quickly forget what they hear. People recall less and less when tested at progressive intervals of one week, three weeks, one month, and three months. By six months—and this is a depressing statistic indeed—98 percent of what listeners have been exposed to is forgotten.[15]

The nugget of good news is that they do remember two percent. If you are clear about your residual message, you get to choose *which* two percent they remember. To maximize your powers of persuasion, make sure you can finish this sentence: "When I am finished speaking I want my audience to believe that _____." This is your residual message.

Stylized Redundancy

Next, boil your speech down to a few main points. Keep these points to no more than three, if you can. Then structure all your evidence so as to bolster these points. Be certain that these central points are obvious to your listeners. Preview them in your introduction, develop them in the body of your speech, and review them in the conclusion. In your introduction, tell your audience what you're going to tell them. In the body of your speech, tell them in detail. In your conclusion, tell them what you've told them.

What's to keep repetition of main points from becoming boring? Stylized redundancy. This means reiterating the main points in different ways. Change the words by which you convey your main points, but keep the meaning unaltered.

Introduction: Three Main Functions

The introduction of your speech serves three main functions:

- It gives the audience a chance to adjust and focus.
- It creates a reason for listening and generates a desire to know more.
- It previews the main points.

The opening tone should be informal so that the audience can settle in and prepare to pay attention. They are getting familiar with you, and you with them.

Now, let the tantalizing begin. Exigence can be created by engaging stories, provocative questions, and surprising statistics. The upshot: Listeners have been served an appetizer that whets their appetite for the main course.

The introduction also serves as an overview in the way that an overture sets the stage for a musical. It should offer up samplings of what's to come by listing the main points you will cover. By the end of the introduction, there should be absolutely no doubt in the minds of listeners as to the speaker's residual message or the main points which drive the message.

Navigating Through the Body of Your Speech

As you navigate through the main part of your talk, you will no doubt have a lot of ideas, information, and supporting evidence to impart. There are two key principles to keep in mind at this juncture. You must have a logical structure that keeps the listener feeling anchored. But you must always be cognizant of the fact that only a bit of what you say—however riveting it is in the here and now—will "stick" in the hereafter.

Keeping the following in mind will help you keep the audience grounded and help you hit your residual message:

Use focus words and cue phrases. Verbally draw attention to what you want the audience to remember. Consider phrases like *"What all this comes down to is"* and *"If you remember nothing else, remember this…."*

Incorporate internal summaries. Let your listeners know where they are in the speech. Where have you taken them so far, and where are you going next? *"So far I've discussed two reasons why we need to change our monetary policy. Now here's a third."* This keeps the audience up to speed, and if people's minds have wandered, it reorients them.

Put agreement before disagreement. It's easiest to gain people's agreement before they have moved into a mode of negativity. Begin with statements with which your audience is likely to concur. For example, you may have a controversial solution to controlling healthcare costs, but before revealing it you can get everyone to agree that healthcare costs are too high. Now listeners are in a "yes" frame of mind.

Address objections. It won't do to pretend that objections to your point of view don't exist. If you believe a substantial portion of your audience has doubts, face these doubts head on, or your efforts will be about as fruitful as throwing seeds into concrete. Acknowledging objections captures the resistance in the audience and raises the chance that you will get your message through. (*"I know that many of you think healthcare costs are out of your control—that you are helpless to change the system. Let me assure you that you do have the power to affect what your family spends on medical care…."*)

Consider a problem/solution structure. If you craft the body of your speech in a problem/solution format, be certain to spend as much time on the solutions as you do on the problem portion. If you spend too much time on the problems, you can overwhelm and unnerve your listeners, leaving them in a state of anxiety. If you spend too much time on the solution phase but fail to develop the problem, the solution seems irrelevant. The problem/solution structure is powerful if both portions are balanced.

Caveat conclusion. The conclusion of a presentation is the easiest thing to get right, but it is also the thing most often gotten wrong. How many times have we heard a presentation conclude with some version of the anticlimactic dud, "Well…that's about it." It's as if the speaker trained for months to run a marathon and then decided to quit right before crossing the finish line.

The rules for making the most of your conclusion are simple and straightforward:

- Reinforce your main points. Quickly and elegantly review the main points that support your residual message.
- End with a forward-looking vision. Leave your listeners with an excited sense of how the future could unfold if they follow your recommendations.
- Conclude on a note of finality. Don't give the impression that you just ran out of things to say.

Here is how Martin Luther King, Jr., ended his breathtaking "I've Been to the Mountaintop" speech, delivered to a crowd of 2,000 in Memphis, Tennessee, the night before he was assassinated in 1968:

"Like anybody, I want to live a long life. Longevity has its place, but I'm not concerned about that now. I just want to do God's will, and He's allowed me to go up to the mountain, and I've looked over and I've seen the Promised Land. I may not get there with you, but I want you to know tonight that we as a people will go to the Promised Land. So I'm happy tonight. I'm not worried.

I'm not worried about anything; I'm not fearing any man. Mine eyes have seen the glory of the coming of the Lord."

Three "Special Effects"

As you know, we've emphasized the paramount importance of the residual message. So we'll conclude the discussion of logos by stressing once again that the lasting influence of your message depends upon your taking multiple opportunities to reiterate this key theme in multiple ways. As you consider how and when to do so, keep in mind these research findings with regard to listener retention:

- Primacy effect—What people hear first they think is significant, and they hold on to.
- Recency effect—What people hear last they think is noteworthy, and they remember.
- Duration effect—What the speaker spends the most time on listeners think is most important, even if it's not.

The practical application of these findings is clear. If you have certain examples, statistics, analogies, and testimonials that are particularly compelling, be sure to put them first (primacy) and last (recency). Avoid going off on lengthy tangents (duration) or you will divert audience attention away from your residual message.

Managing Questions and Answers

Contrary to popular belief, if there is a question and answer period, it should happen *before* your conclusion, *not after*. Any number of things can detract from your residual message if you do things the other way around. You may be asked questions that steer you off the point of your central topic—if indeed they have anything to do with your topic at all. Audience members may grandstand and attempt to get into protracted debates with you. Or you may simply lose listener interest if questions go on too long, or are difficult to hear or understand. In the latter case, you could face the demoralizing sight of audience members tiptoeing out in a trickle that becomes a steady stream. Talk about an anticlimax!

To avoid such debacles, let your audience know that you'll take a limited number of questions before your concluding remarks. Then proceed with these guidelines in mind:

- If you've left time for questions and there are none, pose questions that other audiences have asked in the past.

- If you don't know the answer to a question, concede any information gaps. What you don't know, you don't know. You won't damage well-established credibility by honestly acknowledging what you don't know. But you would damage it by faking an answer.

- If you receive a question that is hostile or a thinly veiled attack, treat the question as if it were helpful. You might say something like, "Ah, I was wondering when someone would raise that very point. Thank you."

- If someone monopolizes the Q&A, using your platform for their soapbox, acknowledge their interest and redirect it:

  Acknowledgment: *"I can see you've thought a lot about this topic, and it has real meaning for you."*

  Redirection: *"It's important for me to move ahead with our agenda, because there's so much to cover."*

  Invitation: *"I'd be delighted to stay afterward and talk with you."* By the way, if this person was merely showing off for the crowd, he or she probably won't stick around.

Preparing Your Presentation

Now that you know the principles of persuasive public speaking, it's essential that you prepare. Many people might set to work creating an outline, but that part of the process should actually follow a more fundamental sort of prep work. First, think back on your past speeches. Evaluate your performance as objectively as possible. How do you think you appeared to your audience? Note areas for improvement and resolve to improve them.

Self-Assessment Summary

Poorly Organized	___	___	___	___ Well Organized
Weak Arguments	___	___	___	___ Strong Arguments
Monotonous	___	___	___	___ Varied
Poor Eye Contact	___	___	___	___ Strong Eye Contact
Stilted Style	___	___	___	___ Conversational
Dull	___	___	___	___ Interesting
Weak	___	___	___	___ Forceful
Indifferent	___	___	___	___ Concerned
Nervous	___	___	___	___ Calm
Disfluent	___	___	___	___ Fluent

Set your targets. Before you do anything else, develop your residual message: When I am finished speaking I want my audience to believe that
_____.

Now answer the question: Who cares? Analyze your listeners and ask yourself why they should care about your message and how hearing it will help them.

Gather your evidence. Ideally, cite examples, statistics, analogies, and testimony from authority.

Begin your outline. Create an introduction that captures listener attention and previews the main points.

Transition to a strategically ordered body that, ideally, includes three main points, each with supporting evidence, and each with a smooth segue to the one following. Remember to use internal summaries ("*Here is where we are so far*") and words that signal the audience to focus on your residual message ("*If you remember nothing else, remember this…*").

Conclude with an elegant, stylized version of your main points, incite the audience to action, and end on a note of finality.

Chapter Ten

Toward a Culture
of Communication

"You can develop the best strategy and technology in the world to take
you from where you are to where you want to go. But in the end,
culture will trump strategy and technology every time."
— *John Haughom, Senior Vice President,
Healthcare Improvement Division, PeaceHealth*

Once you start applying the models and principles for unraveling
the paradoxes of persuasion, you will quickly notice that they're
inextricably interconnected. Before too long, you will instinctively find
yourself synthesizing all of the skills, transitioning seamlessly from one
to another, as new habits of positive persuasion and influence replace
outmoded communication patterns. That's because at the heart of all
the skills we teach—aligning intent and impact, checking perceptions,
responding to criticism, raising delicate issues, fostering collaboration,
respecting and meeting the needs of an audience—there lies one essential unifying fundamental. That fundamental is *the ability to listen*.

As individuals make listening their new default mode—replacing the "waiting for my turn to talk" mindset—astonishing things begin to happen. Problems get solved *and* relationships get better. So often we are asked, "How will I know if I'm doing it right?" This is how. When you see problems resolving and relationships improving, you should view this as a pivotal benchmark in your progress.

Benchmark for Success # 1:
Problems are getting solved and relationships are getting better.

What Happens Next

When individuals within a system—be it a business organization, a community organization, or a family—reach the first benchmark, another amazing dynamic starts to take place as well. The very culture—the underlying social and emotional milieu in which these individuals' relationships function—begins to alter. Within the framework of a culture, learning spreads spontaneously and contagiously from person to person. As the spread occurs, the group as a whole takes on shared patterns of thought and behavior. A kind of conjoint consciousness is formed.

When individuals begin to communicate more effectively, the overall culture becomes more effective. When individuals begin to communicate more positively, the culture becomes more positive. The changes then become self-reinforcing. In lieu of atmospheres where silence, denial, or blame are the norms, customs of constructive communication emerge.

We started talking about the immense impact of culture on organizations and outcomes many years ago. At first, some people said they regarded culture as the "soft stuff." Outcomes, they insisted, depended upon strategic planning. It was goal setting and productivity that would determine end results. Today, however—after the Challenger, after the Columbia, and after the disastrously disorganized response to 9/11—few fail to recognize that outcomes would have been dramatically different had healthy cultures of communication been in place. Moreover, with so many studies documenting the sheer return on investment that business enterprises reap when they invest in fostering constructive communication, training and ongoing research in this area are valued more with every passing year.

With increasing frequency, individuals ask us what they can do within their businesses, their institutions, and their families to help evolve a culture of communication. This is what we tell them.

Put a Communication Infrastructure in Place

In communication, as in all things, first things need to be addressed first. If your goal is to encourage communication within an organization, you already know *why*. But you still need to determine *how*.

How do people communicate within your organization? Are regular times set aside for exchanging ideas and information? How is nonroutine communication initiated, and who is empowered to initiate it? How are ideas and information that come out of your organization exchanged with other, interdependent organizations? Who takes responsibility for that process?

The goal of this kind of evaluation is to understand whether or not the communication infrastructure is functioning smoothly under everyday circumstances. If it's not, the time to enhance the infrastructure is *now*. Any shortcomings—any gaps in the system, any groups or individuals who are left out of the loop, any unresolved conflicts about "who's in charge"—need to be tackled *before* a critical situation comes along to tax a system that is functioning less than optimally.

Henry Kissinger once quipped, "There can't be a crisis next week. My schedule is already full." But, of course, no individual or group of individuals can anticipate what the nature of a crisis will be or when it will arise. The very nature of crisis is that it manifests in ways no one ever expects, and always at "the worst possible moment." The one thing we can all know for certain is that, sooner or later, some sort of crisis—or, at the very least, a potential crisis—will arise. When it does, we must react quickly and resourcefully. The last thing we need to do is waste valuable time as we fail to connect with others whose assistance and cooperation are required. That's the part that should be simple. Imagine the difference in preparedness between people who have pre-programmed the number of their local police and fire departments into their telephone versus people who realize, in mid-fire or mid-burglary, that they need to hunt around for the number—or are not even sure whom to call for help.

How will you know when your organization has a smoothly functioning communication infrastructure? When you no longer have to think about it. When clear lines of communication are firmly established, when communication protocols are clear, when information sharing between individuals and across groups has become an effortless day-to-day event—you will know that you have done the job. Then, when norms are challenged by abnormal events, your infrastructure will be part of the solution rather than part of the problem.

Benchmark for Success # 2:

The communication infrastructure is part of the solution, not part of the problem.

Leader Insight 10-1 shows how a strong communication infrastructure among government agencies helped to avert a crisis.

Leader Insight 10-1

A Crisis Averted by Communication Planning

In 1981, a cult led by controversial self-proclaimed guru Bhagwan Shree Rajneesh purchased a dilapidated 64,000-acre ranch in rural Wasco County, Oregon. The ranch's community of several thousand orange-robed disciples soon took over the nearby town of Antelope, and sought to control the entire county by winning the local election in 1984. Rajneesh was ultimately deported from Oregon under a bevy of serious criminal charges against him and his key followers.

Dave Frohnmayer, then attorney general of Oregon, talked about the coordinated effort it took to investigate and prosecute Rajneesh and his followers without creating what could easily have become a Ruby Ridge or Waco-like debacle. "This was a very sensitive situation," he explained. "We didn't want anyone hurt, and we didn't want to upset the larger population of Oregon or to encourage vigilantism. Our plan to remove Rajneesh was a limited surgical strategy. And because the effort involved half a dozen regulatory agencies at the local, state, and federal level, there needed to be an extraordinary amount of collaboration and coordination."

Communication across the federal, state, and local law enforcement agencies was critical to success, Frohnmayer said. "During the crisis, our office held daily five-way conference calls with the Governor's Office and all of the involved agencies, one in the morning, and again at 4:30 in the afternoon. We wanted to accelerate the degree to which information was shared on the investigative end. We also needed to stay on message in terms of letting the public know that we had no intention of depriving anyone of freedom of religion, nor of harming people or destroying property. We discussed how we would get our message out and what our talking points would be. We also discussed and resolved questions of jurisdiction and agency cooperation. Within this network, no one had the title of chief. Cooperation was based on mutual respect."

An essential element in the eventual success of the collaborative effort was preparedness, Frohnmayer noted. Because of a prior communication initiative undertaken by the office of the attorney general, most of the network and its protocols were in place long before any dire situation arose.

"I am a firm believer in establishing your communication processes before you're in a time of crisis," said Frohnmayer. "Otherwise, you have to learn to communicate when you have really critical messages to get across to each other. That is a much more difficult proposition. The key is to establish the patterns beforehand."

Let Communication Flow in All Directions

To foster a true culture of communication, it's also necessary to ensure that dialogue and information flow in every direction and that dialogues are facilitated. Most organizations find it relatively easy to disperse information in a top-down direction. When leadership wants to say something, there are already numerous mechanisms in place for getting that message out. Moreover, everyone is expected to pay attention to messages that come down from above. After all, "above"—the realm of bosses, committee chairpersons, parents, and the like—tends to control the power base.

Numerous forces, however, conspire to make it difficult for information to move in an upward direction. People at the top often don't wish to hear from the "rank and file," even if they say they do. And systems are often not in place to facilitate bottom-to-top communication. Even in cases where those at the top genuinely do wish to listen, and have put systems in place to empower those who wish to communicate with them, people lower in the hierarchy may be reluctant to speak out. They're afraid of courting disfavor and jeopardizing their security. The rank and file may complain to one another if they perceive a problem at the top, but those at the top too often remain oblivious.

Organizations also find it difficult to facilitate the lateral flow of communication. In many companies, the most deficient kind of communication is that which takes place—or, more correctly, does *not* take place—between various departments, divisions, and business units. Groups within organizations are likely to take complaints about other groups anywhere and everywhere but directly to the group with whom they have an issue.

Finally, many organizations have a hard time soliciting information from groups or individuals outside their own ranks. Though much time and effort may be put into soliciting feedback from customers, business partners, community stakeholders, and the like, offering thoughtful feedback takes time—and many people are not in the habit of devoting their time to a constructive feedback process. They will, however, complain to just about anyone else who will listen that the organization is unresponsive.

What all of these difficulties add up to is a tremendous amount of indirect communication—communication that circles around and wafts about and goes everywhere but where it should. Ideally, communication should take the shortest possible route. In an effective, empowering culture of communication, people go directly to the source of a problem in order to resolve it.

Benchmark for Success # 3:

People go directly to the source of a problem in order to resolve it.

In Leader Insight 10-2, a large city seeks to implement such a culture in order to realize its mission.

Leader Insight 10-2

A City with a Vision: Thriving on Feedback

Edinburgh, Scotland, is a city with a mission. "Its half million citizens," says Chief Executive Tom Aitchison, "want Edinburgh to be the best city in Northern Europe by 2015." The Chief Executive believes that this can be accomplished by creating a coalition of public-and-private-sector interests and by facilitating communication. To this end, Edinburgh is implementing a new Community Plan, the success of which will depend upon how well it gets major stakeholders to engage.

"Edinburgh is a thriving commercial, financial, and tourism city. The business community in particular doesn't like to waste time with needless meetings. So," Aitchison says, "communication processes must be slick and efficient. Feedback from all sections of the community is vitally important, and we want to engage with those 'hard to reach' groups, as well as those who regularly respond to consultation exercises."

Commit to Constructive Language

Most important of all, a culture that values the power of communication will operate from the premise that *everyone* is responsible for perpetuating this consummate value. All members of the organization are expected to communicate directly with one another, to listen carefully and nonjudgmentally, and to craft messages that are helpful and beneficial to those who receive them.

In a healthy culture, ambiguities are rare. Intent aligns with impact, and content is free of blame, baiting, backbiting, buck-passing, and Monday-morning quarterbacking. In this type of culture, people are expected to acknowledge and address problems, and also to reinforce one another's successes.

Is this an ideal that's easy to achieve? Of course not. Some people are reluctant to view communication as anything other than a means of furthering their own agendas. We should also note that technological advances sometimes serve to perpetuate negative communication modes. These days, for example, we routinely hear sordid tales of email abuse.

People are prone to saying things in an email they would never say in person or even over the telephone, because the impersonal, once-removed process of email spares them from having to see or hear a recipient's reaction. To make matters worse, senders of inflammatory emails will often copy their message to a multitude of other unwitting "witnesses," as an underhanded way of subgrouping and factionalizing. The result is that the recipient feels sand-bagged and ganged up on before having a chance to respond.

Email isn't going to go away, of course, nor should it. If used properly it can streamline collaboration and serve as a means of initiating widespread, thoughtful feedback. But every new medium will bring with it new challenges, and a culture of communication must be watchful of its impact. As new media are integrated into the communication infrastructure, new training and agreements must take place.

A culture in which everyone communicates flawlessly at all times is probably an unrepresentative ideal. But in a culture that genuinely understands the immense benefit of constructive communication, those people who are viewed as positive, persuasive communicators become role models. They represent the standard to which everyone aspires.

Benchmark for Success # 4:
Positive, persuasive communicators become role models.

In Leader Insight 10-3, we see how a positive role model turned a large company's culture—and profits—around.

Leader Insight 10-3

Language Fuels a Cultural Sea Change, a Business Turnaround

When Wayne Norrie and partner Roger Cockayne purchased 51% of Hitachi Data Systems, New Zealand, the company went from losing money to becoming one of the most phenomenal turnaround stories in New Zealand. Norrie's self-proclaimed title tells much about the success. Wayne is Chief Executive Officer and Minister of Culture. His credo: Have everyone take ownership, accountability, and responsibility. The company activates this concept by empowering all employees to announce to each other when they see someone operating "below the line"—i.e., indulging in blame, excuses, or denial.

"When new employees join the company, they go through a 'rock ceremony,'" Norrie says. "They receive a rock with their name on it—the rock of honesty. This rock is brought to bi-annual rock meetings, the purpose of which is to clear the air in a ritualistic truth-telling session where people attack the hard issues head on."

At such meetings, and at all other times, members of the organization are encouraged to apply a Say It Positively (SIP) standard. "Language is the framework of thoughts," Norrie says. "Thoughts drive action; action drives results. Language determines the glasses you wear, what you see and experience. Positive language creates a positive lens. If someone asks, 'How's your day going?' and you say, 'Not bad,' that's two negatives. Now think about the impact if you reply, 'Awesome, thanks.'"

To keep people focused on the positive, Norrie begins routine meetings with sixty seconds for staffers to list twenty accomplishments. Once again, language impacts perception. "Small tasks completed now turn into accomplishments. People feel positively about what they've done and what they can do.

"The overall lesson," Norrie says, "is that *you* control your emotions even though you can't control external events. How you experience an event is always your choice. To opt for blame, excuses, and denial is to be a victim. To choose accountability and responsibility is to be a victor."

Hitachi saw a 40-percent surge in revenue in the first year of its Say It Positively culture, and a 100-percent improvement in EBIT (earnings before interest and taxes) income the following year. "We know these changes are attributable to culture," says Norrie, "because only our culture changed. Everything else stayed the same—the staff, customers, suppliers, and producers.

"You are only as good as your company's culture allows your people to be," Norrie concludes. "Culture is not an amorphous entity. It's the single greatest asset to organizational performance."

Implement Realistic Criteria

Complementary to three of the preceding benchmarks—putting a communication infrastructure in place, letting communication flow in all directions, and committing to constructive language—is a focus on instituting these changes in such a way that they can be evaluated. It's one thing to say *we will talk to one another*; it's another to stipulate when and for how long everyone will talk. In the latter case, talking to one another is not a vague ideal, but a tangible action that can be monitored. Did we hold that meeting each and every week? Were concrete ideas exchanged? What were the decisions made in those meetings, and what were the outcomes of those decisions? Were these decisions communicated to key stakeholders?

Organizational goals of *facilitating honesty* or *generating respectfulness* sound laudable and are hard to quibble with (indeed only a Grinch would do so), but such dictates are also hard to follow up on. Organizations that are serious about creating and enhancing a culture of communication will specify the exact steps that will be taken in support of that goal.

Benchmark for Success # 5:
Tangible criteria are set for measuring the results of change.

What if My Organization Won't Change?

Not everyone will be fortunate enough to be part of an organization that embraces a culture of communication. It can be an extremely frustrating experience to be among the first to be convinced of the importance of something, even when you believe deep down that others will ultimately follow. Still, there's no need to throw up your hands, and no reason to stop acquiring the new habits you know will yield such valuable results.

Remember, a communication system will begin to change *if even one single aspect of it alters*. Gradually but steadfastly, all the other pieces of a system will adapt to accommodate the shift that's already occurred. Gandhi said, "Be the change you wish to see in the world." You can be the change in your culture—in your company, in your community, in your family. You can be the influential communicator that becomes the role model for others.

Be Quiet, Be Heard: A Mantra for Life

We don't mean to imply that your path will be easy or effortless, or that you won't experience setbacks. There will doubtless be occasions when exceptional stress plunges you briefly back into old habits. You will, from time to time, encounter especially challenging people who are slower than others to respond to your new methods of influencing and persuading. When that happens, you may feel like you can't recall much of anything from your new communication repertoire. That's okay. At moments that try your memory, your patience, and even your soul, all you need to remember are four words: *Be Quiet, Be Heard*.

Let this phrase be your mantra—a snippet of self-talk that instantly alters your frame of mind. Say *Be Quiet, Be Heard* to yourself whenever you feel you are about to revert to an old habit of accusation, denial, or reflexive self-defense. The *be quiet* part will serve as a thought-stopper, a device which—as research in the field of cognitive behavior modification tells us—can serve to interrupt the typical pattern of negative thinking. But *Be Quiet, Be Heard* goes beyond stopping thoughts—to restarting them in a new direction. Repeating this phrase silently to yourself will provide a powerful reminder that by holding your tongue you will, paradoxically, be better able to influence and persuade. By holding your tongue, you may, paradoxically, be the most powerful person in the room.

Remember to keep your eye on the first benchmark. You will know that you are doing it right *because problems will begin to be solved and relationships will improve.*

Where should you start? Start anywhere. Start with anyone. You can rest assured that within hours of finishing this book, perhaps even within moments, someone is going to try to tell you something. We can't tell you what that person's message will be. We can't tell you what it means or how to respond to it so that person feels heard and understood. But *you* will know, and you will be on your way. All you really need to do is listen.

Notes

Introduction

1. Aristotle's *Rhetoric* dates back to 350 B.C. For a current edition, see the translation by Hugh Lawson-Tancred (Penguin Classics, 1992).

2. Robert Bianco, "Ellen 'Shines' – Sharon 'Shrieks,'" *USA Today* 17 Sept. 2003: 3D.

Chapter 1

3. The Watson Wyatt™ Worldwide material is quoted from *Connecting Organizational Communication to Financial Performance*: 2003/2004 Communication ROI Study.

4. The statistic on health clubs was quoted in the American Cancer Society's *Workplace Services* newsletter, January 2004: 1.

Chapter 2

5. For a detailed discussion of facial expressions, including micro-expressions, see the work of Dr. Paul Ekman, creator of the Facial Action Coding System. Paul Ekman, *Emotions Revealed: Recognizing Faces and Feelings to Improve Communication and Emotional Life* (New York City: Henry Holt & Company, 2003).

6. Interpersonal expectancy in the classroom is detailed in R. Rosenthal and L. Jacobsen, *Pygmalion in the Classroom* (New York City: Holt, Rinehart & Winston, 1968).

Chapter 3

7. The "see>think>feel>want>do" module is adapted from Sherod Miller, Elam W. Nunally, Daniel B. Wackman, Robert Friederichsen, *Alive and Aware: Improving Communication in Relationships* (Interpersonal Communication Programs, Incorporated, 1975).

Chapter 6

8. For more information on positive psychology, see Martin Seligman, *Authentic Happiness: Using the New Positive Psychology to Realize Your Potential for Lasting Fulfillment* (New York City: Free Press, 2002).

Chapter 7

9. Susan R. Glaser, "Teamwork and Communication: A Three-Year Case Study of Change," *Management Communication Quarterly* 7.3 (1994): 282-96.

10. The NASA review panel findings were posted on the Spaceflight Now Web site on March 14, 2000, and were reported by CBS and *Washington Post* consultant Willliam Harwood. The report of the Presidential Commission on the Space Shuttle Challenger Accident (1986) and the Implementation of the Recommendations of the Presidential Commission on the Space Shuttle Challenger Accident (1987) can be found at the Web site of the National Aeronautics and Space Administration (www.nasa.gov).

11. For more information on appreciative inquiry, see James Magruder Watkins and Bernard J. Mohr, *Appreciative Inquiry* (San Francisco, CA: Jossey-Bass Pfeiffer, 2001) and Diana Whitney and Amanda Trosten-Bloom, *The Power of Appreciative Inquiry* (San Francisco, CA: Berrett-Koehler Publishers, 2003).

Chapter 8

12. In a study by the market research firm R.H. Bruskin Associates (1973), participants ranked the things they feared most. Snakes came in at number three; dying at number two. The number one fear was the fear of public speaking.

Chapter 9

13. The ancient text *The Maxims of Ptah-hotep* was recovered for the world in the 1840s by a French Egyptologist.

14. For more information on rate-of-speech data, see Stephen E. Lucas, *The Art of Public Speaking* (New York City: McGraw Hill, 2001).

15. For more information on retentions studies, see Gerald M. Phillips and J. Jerome Zolten, *Structuring Speech* (New York City: Bobbs-Merrill, 1976).

Be Quiet, Be Heard
Order Form

Fax Orders: 541-343-1706
Telephone Orders: 800-980-0321
Email Orders: info@theglasers.com
Website: www.theglasers.com
Postal Orders: Communication Solutions Publishing
Executive Offices
1740 Craigmont Ave, Eugene, OR 97405
USA

Please send me *Be Quiet, Be Heard* _____ copies @ $18.95 each
(For information about group orders, please contact 541-343-7575)

Subtotal: _____

• Shipping: _____

Total: _____

Enclosed: _____

• *$5.00 for first book, $2.00 for each additional book.*
  International: US $10.00 for first book, $5.00 for each additional book.

(Please print)
Name: _____

Address: _____

City: _____ State: _____

Postal Code: _____ Country: _____

Phone: _____

Email: _____

Payment: ❏Check enclosed   ❏Visa   ❏Mastercard   ❏PayPal

Card Number : _____

Name on Card : _____ Exp. Date:___ /_____

✧

Be Quiet, Be Heard
Order Form

Fax Orders: 541-343-1706
Telephone Orders: 800-980-0321
Email Orders: info@theglasers.com
Website: www.theglasers.com
Postal Orders: Communication Solutions Publishing
Executive Offices
1740 Craigmont Ave, Eugene, OR 97405
USA

Please send me *Be Quiet, Be Heard* _____ copies @ $18.95 each
(For information about group orders, please contact 541-343-7575)

Subtotal: _____

• Shipping: _____

Total: _____

Enclosed: _____

• *$5.00 for first book, $2.00 for each additional book.*
  International: US $10.00 for first book, $5.00 for each additional book.

(Please print)
Name: _____

Address: _____

City: _____ State: _____

Postal Code: _____ Country: _____

Phone: _____

Email: _____

Payment: ❑Check enclosed   ❑Visa   ❑Mastercard   ❑PayPal

Card Number : _____

Name on Card : _____ Exp. Date:___ /_____